MANAGING THE PUBLIC HEALTH ENTERPRISE

Edited by

Edward L. Baker, Jr., MD, MPH

Research Professor and Director
North Carolina Institute for Public Health
University of North Carolina
Gillings School of Global Public Health
Chapel Hill, North Carolina

Anne J. Menkens, PhD

Program Director
Office of Executive Education
North Carolina Institute for Public Health
Chapel Hill, North Carolina

Janet E. Porter, PhD

Executive Vice President/Chief Operating Officer
Dana-Farber Cancer Institute
and
Deputy Director
Dana-Farber/Brigham and Women's Cancer Center
Boston, Massachusetts

D1082046

JONES AND BARTLETT PUBLISHERS
Sudbury, Massachusetts
BOSTON   TORONTO   LONDON   SINGAPORE

World Headquarters

Jones and Bartlett Publishers	Jones and Bartlett Publishers	Jones and Bartlett Publishers
40 Tall Pine Drive	Canada	International
Sudbury, MA 01776	6339 Ormindale Way	Barb House, Barb Mews
978-443-5000	Mississauga, Ontario L5V 1J2	London W6 7PA
info@jbpub.com	Canada	United Kingdom
www.jbpub.com		

Jones and Bartlett's books and products are available through most bookstores and online booksellers. To contact Jones and Bartlett Publishers directly, call 800-832-0034, fax 978-443-8000, or visit our website, www.jbpub.com.

Substantial discounts on bulk quantities of Jones and Bartlett's publications are available to corporations, professional associations, and other qualified organizations. For details and specific discount information, contact the special sales department at Jones and Bartlett via the above contact information or send an email to specialsales@jbpub.com.

This publication is designed to provide accurate and authoritative information in regard to the Subject Matter covered. It is sold with the understanding that the publisher is not engaged in rendering legal, accounting, or other professional service. If legal advice or other expert assistance is required, the service of a competent professional person should be sought.

Production Credits
Publisher: Michael Brown
Production Director: Amy Rose
Associate Editor: Katey Birtcher
Editorial Assistant: Catie Heverling
Senior Production Editor: Tracey Chapman
Associate Production Editor: Kate Stein
Marketing Manager: Sophie Fleck
Associate Marketing Manager: Jessica Cormier
Manufacturing and Inventory Control Supervisor: Amy Bacus
Composition: Achorn International
Art: Accurate Art, Inc.
Cover Design: Scott Moden
Cover and Opener Image: © Victoria Field/ShutterStock, Inc.
Printing and Binding: Malloy, Inc.
Cover Printing: Malloy, Inc.

Library of Congress Cataloging-in-Publication Data
Managing the public health enterprise / [edited by] Edward Baker, Anne Menkens, and Janet Porter.
    p. ; cm.
  Includes bibliographical references and index.
  ISBN 978-0-7637-6382-4 (pbk.)
  1. Public health administration. I. Baker, Edward L. II. Menkens, Anne J. III. Porter, Janet.
  [DNLM: 1. Public Health Administration. WA 525 M2665 2010]
  RA427.M36 2010
  362.1068—dc22

                                  2008054202

6048

Printed in the United States of America
13 12 11 10 09   10 9 8 7 6 5 4 3 2 1

Dedication

To Pam, Justin, Ryan, and Lindsay.
—E.L.B.

To JAE, whose commitment to public health and dedication to good writing are truly inspirational. Thank you for your support and friendship.
—A.J.M.

To my parents, Myrna Dible Porter, who passed on her passion for public health nursing, and Hugh Fredrick Porter, who instilled in me a strong work ethic and desire to lead.
—J.E.P.

Contents

Foreword

Making a Difference through Public Health Management

Much of my career has been spent advocating preventive public health. Studies show that life expectancy in the United States grew from 45 in 1900 to around 80 today. It has been demonstrated that 30 of those years gained are attributable to preventive activities, with the remaining five associated with advances in treatment. And those preventive activities had to be applied at the population level to affect a demographic variable such as life expectancy.

Public health managers lead the organizations that have helped make these advances possible. Every day, public health managers run the programs and provide the services that lead to better health and safety for us all. Furthermore, they deal with management challenges for which they may not have been trained.

This book is for those busy public health managers. The work is a collection of new and previously published articles from the

"Management Moment" column, a regular piece in the *Journal of Public Health Management and Practice*, which provides commentary and practical guidance on management issues commonly encountered in public health practice. Today's public health manager must keep both the big picture and the details in mind to envision new projects and run long-standing ones. While looking out for the next SARS or avian flu outbreak, the next hurricane or terrorist attack, while testing well water and immunizing babies, the public health manager must balance budgets, hire personnel, run meetings, communicate with staff and partners, learn to use new technology, and find funding, all within the context of turbulent economic times, new and re-emerging health and safety threats, and a growing burden of chronic disease.

Managing the Public Health Enterprise contains concrete advice for these management challenges. It is an excellent tool for people in the field, in public health or in other management situations—a refresher, perhaps, for seasoned veterans, and a source of information and inspiration for those just starting their careers. Individuals might want to use it to handle particular problems that arise, and leaders might want to use it to spur discussion within teams or for individual development activities for staff. The book is practical and clear. It is broad in scope and yet focused on timely matters at hand, and the range of perspectives make it enjoyable and relevant to a broad audience.

The concepts raised and suggestions offered in this book will help today's public health managers lead their organizations, and their communities, to conquer tomorrow's health challenges.

William L. Roper, MD, MPH
CEO, University of North Carolina
Health Care System
Vice Chancellor for Medical Affairs
Dean, University of North Carolina
School of Medicine

Looking Inward: Better Management for Better Public Health

So much of our work in public health is outward looking. The challenges and opportunities that we face increasingly have effects beyond our local, state, and even national boundaries. With this truth in mind, however, it is important not to forget the significance of looking inward: examining and improving how we run our local health departments and, specifically, how we as individuals manage the relationships we have with internal and external colleagues and partners; how we manage the information we share and disseminate; and how we manage to fund and sustain our public health enterprise in uncertain economic times.

Developing management is a fundamental part of improving the public's health, and the essays in this volume present the tools and strategies to help us get there. Some of the articles have been published previously, in the *Journal of Public Health Management and Practice*; others are new to this volume. All present practical advice for today's public health manager. The reader will find a diversity of voices, wide-ranging cases to illustrate the practical points, and a little bit of theory. Most important, this book presents ways to think concretely about the things we do to make the organization run smoothly, so that the work we do can have the best—and broadest—impact on population health.

> Barbara K. Rimer, DrPH
> Dean and Alumni Distinguished Professor
> University of North Carolina
> Gillings School of Global Public Health

Acknowledgments

We would like to acknowledge some people whose work and advocacy have made this book possible.

First, Dr. Lloyd Novick has been an invaluable ally in this project, offering both practical guidance to us and inspiration and leadership to the field as a whole. Dr. Novick is a pillar in the field of public health practice, known for his work as a leader of statewide health agencies, as a professor and program director of preventive medicine (currently leading the Division of Community Health and Preventive Medicine and master's program in public health at East Carolina University), and as the author or editor of several books, including the most widely used textbook in public health administration. Individuals at every level of public health practice turn to his *Journal of Public Health Management and Practice*, in which we first published many of these chapters. We are thankful for his support of our work.

We also wish to acknowledge Dr. Bill Roper. Dr. Roper has been a major supporter of efforts to improve public health management in the United States for decades and is an inspiration to both healthcare and public health professionals. A pediatrician by training, Bill Roper began his public health career as a local public health director in Birmingham, Alabama. When he later served as director of the Centers for Disease Control and Prevention, Dr. Roper made strengthening the public health system a priority, including giving managers and leaders the skills they needed to face the challenges of a new millennium. He continued to light our way as dean of our School of Public Health and is now dean of the University of North Carolina School of Medicine, CEO of UNC Health Care, and vice chancellor for Medical Affairs.

Third, we'd like to thank our contributing authors, whose contributions show forth their great dedication to the field of public health management development. They include our colleagues at the Dana Farber Cancer Institute, whose work ensures that the crucial conversation between healthcare and public health professionals continues. They also include our colleagues here at the University of North Carolina at Chapel Hill—at the North Carolina Institute for Public Health, the Gillings School of Global Public Health, the Kenan-Flagler Business School, and the Medical Foundation of North Carolina. All of these individuals generously shared their expertise and knowledge to help us advance knowledge in the field about essential public health management competencies.

Finally, to our students, colleagues, and audience—the public health practitioners who have informed our knowledge on these topics and who have let us know over the years that our work is valuable to them in their day-to-day working lives. Their feedback and support have given us the confidence that these lessons truly relate to people in the field. You make this book possible.

About the Authors

Edward L. Baker, Jr. serves as director of the North Carolina Institute for Public Health (NCIPH), the outreach and service unit of the University of the North Carolina Gillings School of Global Public Health. He is also a professor in the Departments of Health Policy and Administration and Epidemiology. He previously served as assistant surgeon general in the U.S. Public Health Service and director of the Centers for Disease Control and Prevention's Public Health Practice Program Office. Initiatives developed under his leadership include the Public Health Leadership Institutes, the Information Network for Public Health Officials, the Public Health Training Network, the Sustainable Management Development Program, the Health Alert Network, the National Public Health Performance Standards Program, the National Laboratory Training Network, and the Management Academy for Public Health. Previously, he served as deputy director of the National Institute for Occupational Safety and Health and on the faculty of Harvard University School of Public Health's Occupational Health Program. Currently, Dr. Baker is the director of the National Public Health Leadership

Institute and the Office of Executive Education within NCIPH. He serves as a senior advisor and faculty for the Caribbean Health Leadership Institute managed by the University of the West Indies. Dr. Baker trained in medicine at Baylor College of Medicine, in public health and occupational health at Harvard, and in preventive medicine and epidemiology at the CDC.

Anne J. Menkens is a program director at the North Carolina Institute for Public Health Office of Executive Education. She has worked in public health education and research communications since 1997 and is responsible for the planning and implementation of Executive Education Alumni programs as well as writing and editing projects for the institute. She is the author, with Stephen N. Orton and Pamela Santos, of *Public Health Business Planning: A Practical Guide* (Jones and Bartlett, 2008). She holds a PhD in English from the University of North Carolina at Chapel Hill.

Janet E. Porter has been a passionate advocate for leadership development throughout her career. She is currently the executive vice president and chief operating officer of Dana-Farber Cancer Institute. Previously she served as associate dean for Executive Education for the School of Public Health at the University of North Carolina at Chapel Hill for seven years. Their leadership programs now have 1,200 professionals in them. Before UNC, Dr. Porter was the chief operating officer for Children's Hospital in Columbus, Ohio, for nine years. She is on the faculties of the University of Minnesota, the University of North Carolina at Chapel Hill, Ohio State University, and Harvard University. Dr. Porter received a Bachelor of Science and Master of Health Administration from Ohio State University and a PhD in strategic management from the University of Minnesota.

About the Contributors

Robert C. Amelio is the vice president of Diversity and Talent Management at Dana-Farber Cancer Institute, where he oversees diversity initiatives, recruiting, workforce development, and learning and organizational development. Prior to joining Dana-Farber, he was the director of diversity, training, and development at Harvard University Medical School. Mr. Amelio has consulted on, developed, and implemented diversity and change initiatives within federal government agencies through the U.S. Office of Personnel Management and in academic settings such as Harvard University; the Moses Brown School in Providence, Rhode Island; and the Weill Medical Center at Cornell University in New York City. Mr. Amelio earned his Master of Social Work from Simmons College and his Master of Arts from Emerson College, both in Boston, Massachusetts. He has been an adjunct faculty member at both schools, as well as at Regis College in Weston, Massachusetts. He is a member of the American Society for Training and Development and the Institute for Diversity in Health Management. He received certification in emotional intelligence and diversity from the Emotional Intelligence and Diversity Institute in Los Angeles in 2005.

Dianne Cerce is a senior healthcare executive with over 30 years of work experience in operations and business and program development in an academic environment. Currently, she is the executive director of the Oncology Services for the Dana-Farber/Brigham and Women's Cancer Center (DF/BWCC). Prior to working for the DF/BWCC, Ms. Cerce served in many senior clinical and financial leadership roles at Brigham and Women's Hospital.

Ms. Cerce earned her Master's Degree in Business Administration from Suffolk University and her Bachelor of Science in Business Administration and Accounting from Northeastern University. She has served on the Board of Boston Med Flight, whose mission is to extend the tertiary care service of the major Boston hospitals to the citizens of Massachusetts and New England. A major accomplishment of this board was to expand transport services from one helicopter to three, and increase the array of services to include provision of fixed wing services. Ms. Cerce is a proud mother of two and has served on various educational boards in her home town of Canton, Massachusetts.

Rebecca Davis is a doctoral candidate in the Department of Health Behavior and Health Education at the University of North Carolina Gillings School of Global Public Health.

Gregory Philip Duyck is a graduate of Carnegie-Mellon University and Emerson College creative writing programs. He began his development career in 1993 at one of the 25 largest U.S. community foundations. He then worked as a grant officer for the Providence School Department before founding Rainmaker Grant Services in 1998. Rainmaker provided grant research, writing, planning, and training services to nonprofits in Rhode Island and Massachusetts through a network of consultants. In 2001, Mr. Duyck became associate director of Development at the Oregon Health and Science University School of Medicine before returning to North Carolina and joining the staff of UNC-Chapel Hill in 2003. At UNC, he has been director of Major Gifts at the UNC School of Public Health, associate director of Corporate and Foundation Relations at the Office of University Development, and in May 2007 took the post of director of Major Gifts at the Medical Foundation of North Carolina.

Claudia S. Plaisted Fernandez is a specialist in developing custom executive education programs that focus on personal leadership development, innovation, and business skills for senior, middle, and front-line managers and leaders. As a licensed and registered dietitian, she has a particular interest in leadership in healthcare systems and high-performing healthcare and public health teams. Currently, she directs the American College of Gynecologists and Obstetricians (ACOG) National Leadership Institute and serves as the leadership core director for the Food Systems Leadership Institute. She has cocreated and/or led several leadership institutes, including the Managing in Turbulent Times: the Kellogg Fellowship for Emerging Leaders in Public Health Program (a minority leadership development program), the Southeast Public Health Leadership Institute, and Leadership Novant for the Novant Healthcare system. She is also a trained hypnotherapist and a specialist in stress management. She has 20 years of experience counseling clients with eating disorders and weight management issues.

Dr. Fernandez earned her Bachelor of Science from Miami University of Ohio and her Master of Science from Boston University. She earned her doctorate in leadership studies from the University of North Carolina at Chapel Hill in 2003. In 2007, she joined the faculty in the Department of Maternal and Child Health at the UNC Gillings School of Global Public Health.

Kimberley Freire is a senior fellow at the CDC Foundation. She works with the Centers for Disease Control and Prevention Division of Violence Prevention on intimate partner violence prevention. Ms. Freire previously worked as a graduate research assistant and program evaluator for the University of North Carolina's Injury Prevention Research Center and the North Carolina Public Health Institute. She received a Master of Public Health at Boston University and a doctorate in Health Behavior and Health Education at the UNC Gillings School of Global Public Health. Ms. Freire's current research interests are in violence prevention, program evaluation, organizational learning, and adolescent health.

James H. Johnson, Jr. is the William R. Kenan Jr. Distinguished Professor of entrepreneurship and director of the Urban Investment Strategies Center at the University of North Carolina Kenan-Flagler Business School. His research interests include community and economic development, the effects of demographic changes on the U.S. workplace, interethnic minority conflict in advanced industrial societies, urban poverty and public policy in urban America, and workforce diversity issues. With support from the Russell Sage Foundation, he is researching the economic impact of September 11 on U.S. metropolitan communities. He has published more than 100 scholarly research articles and three research monographs and has coedited four theme issues of scholarly journals on these and related topics. His latest book is *Prismatic Metropolis: Inequality in Los Angeles*. He received his PhD from Michigan

State University, his Master of Science from the University of Wisconsin, Madison, and his Bachelor of Science from North Carolina Central University.

Darlene Lewis is senior vice president for Human Resources at Dana-Farber Cancer Institute. In this role, she helps guide hiring, retention, employee relations, and professional development policies for the institute's staff of roughly 3300, including caregivers, scientists, administrators, and support employees. Previously, Dr. Lewis served as vice president and chief human resources officer at the University of Chicago Medical Center; she has held similar positions at Vanderbilt University and Medical Center in Nashville and the University of Pittsburgh Magee-Womens Hospital. Dr. Lewis also served as Massachusetts Governor Michael Dukakis's deputy commissioner of Administration and Finance for three years, as a corporate human resource manager for Tandon Corporation in California, and as an office systems specialist with Johnson and Higgins in Japan. She earned a PhD in organizational development from Benedictine University in 2007 and holds an Master of Science from the University of Illinois, Urbana-Champaign, and a Bachelor of Arts from San Diego State University.

Tracy Lockard is the business process director for the Cabarrus Health Alliance, the Public Health Authority of Cabarrus County, North Carolina. In this role, she manages the agency's work associated with the Robert Wood Johnson Foundation Common Ground grant and provides expertise in business process analysis, business process redesign, and requirements definition for information systems and business improvement projects. Most recently, Ms. Lockard directed a project to develop requirements for a practice management/electronic medical records system, facilitating collaborative meetings with nine divisions and seven regional North Carolina public health departments. Prior to joining the Alliance, Ms. Lockard spent 15 years working for several high-tech companies in product management, marketing, and business development roles, creating strategic business and marketing plans, developing and launching new and existing products, and building processes and procedures. She holds a Bachelor of Arts in Communications from the University of Kentucky, a certification in Software Product Management from the University of Washington, and completed the Management Academy for Public Health program at the University of North Carolina at Chapel Hill.

Stephen N. Orton is deputy director of the Office of Executive Education at the North Carolina Institute for Public Health, the service and outreach arm of the UNC Gillings School of Global Public Health. Dr. Orton also holds an adjunct assistant professor appointment in the

Health Policy and Administration Department. He has worked in public health executive education since 1994; he was the first program manager for the Management Academy for Public Health in 1999. He has published several articles and is a coauthor of *Public Health Business Planning: A Practical Guide*. He earned his PhD in English from the University of North Carolina at Chapel Hill in 1998.

Amy Porter-Tacoronte is vice president of Operations at Dana-Farber Cancer Institute, where she is primarily responsible for directing and overseeing clinic operations related to patient flow, patient and provider scheduling, clinic financial management, and quality improvement measures. She is also a member of the DFCI Operating Council, which supports and directs operating processes and performance throughout the organization; serves as executive sponsor for the Employees of Color Resource Group; and conducts annual institute time management and career development training for administrative staff. In previous positions, Ms. Porter-Tacoronte served as a business manager and quality improvement project manager at Massachusetts General Hospital and a healthcare consultant at Feeley and Driscoll. At Dana-Farber, she has served as a program administrator and then administrative director of research and clinical operations in the thoracic and gastrointestinal oncology programs and as chief administrator for the Department of Medical Oncology. Ms. Porter-Tacoronte received a Bachelor of Science in applied anatomy and physiology with a minor in business management.

Karl Umble is program planner and evaluator and distance education specialist at the North Carolina Institute for Public Health and the University of North Carolina at Chapel Hill Gillings School of Global Public Health. He plans and evaluates executive education, continuing education, and distance learning programs, and teaches program evaluation. He currently works with the Management Academy for Public Health, the National and Southeastern Public Health Leadership Institutes, Emerging Leaders in Public Health, the Caribbean Health Leadership Institute, and other programs. Dr. Umble's previous positions include health educator with the Virginia Department of Health, where he trained field staff, designed programs, conducted evaluations, and wrote proposals. While obtaining his PhD, he consulted in training evaluation with the Centers for Disease Control and Prevention. Dr. Umble's publications have appeared in several top journals in the fields of public health, health care, and evaluation. Umble is a member of the Academy of Human Resource Development, the American Evaluation Association, and the American Public Health Association. Dr. Umble received a Master of Public Health in Health Behavior and Education from the University of Alabama at Birmingham School of Public Health and a PhD in Adult Education from the University of Georgia.

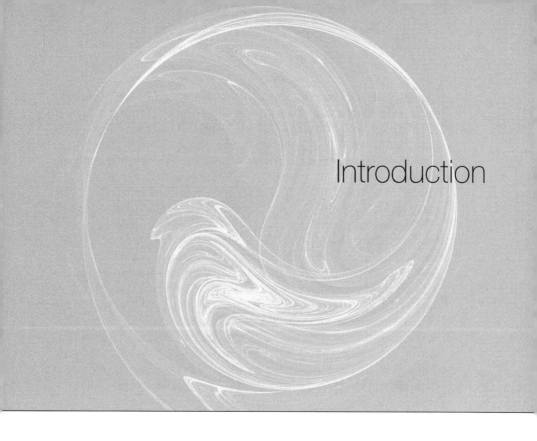

Introduction

Why Public Health *Management*?

Our goal in this book is to provide public health managers with something they can use, something that will help them when they receive the feedback "She doesn't listen to me" (from a subordinate), or "He should be more proactive with handling staff problems" (from a superior). We wish to contribute something to turn to when a new project is presented: when you have to figure out how to fund the new mobile flu vaccination unit, form a team to implement new human resources policies, find a community partner to help address the obesity problem in children, explain to the media why the sewage treatment plant failed during the spring flood, and what you are going to do next time to prevent such an event . . . or *whatever*—because you know as well as we do how difficult it is to anticipate everything that will come your way as a manager of a public health agency.

Or, maybe you don't. Maybe you are just starting out, or are still a student or moving up through the ranks hoping to have the top job some day. Maybe you work in another industry and dream of moving over to the public health realm. Or, maybe you work for a partner organization who just wants to understand the inner workings of the local health department, the way public health practitioners think, what their concerns and challenges are. In any of these cases, this book is for you, too.

Many of the chapters in this book are reprinted articles from the "Management Moment" column of the *Journal of Public Health Management and Practice*, with permission of the publisher and with encouragement from Dr. Lloyd Novick, who has so ably edited the journal for many years. The *Journal of Public Health Management and Practice* is a leading peer-reviewed journal that provides practice-based information applicable to the design and implementation of public health programs. Managers have to design and implement programs every day, and they turn to the journal to see what works and what does not. But a lot of what public health managers do is *manage*—they manage staff, manage external relationships, manage money and resources, manage communication at all different levels and for different purposes. This book speaks to this gap in public health education and professional development.

Why *Public Health* Management?

Although the tasks may be similar, public health management is different from other management positions in some important ways. For one thing, public health managers generally lead governmental organizations, which says a lot about the money streams they work with (not always gushing and often strictly controlled), the organizational culture they can expect (not necessarily open to innovation or change), who their stakeholders are (everybody, to some extent), and how they make decisions (or decisions are made for them) on a daily basis. Also, few public health managers are actually trained in public health. That means managers have little or no training often in the very field they are overseeing—or in management more generally; this lack of educational preparation may be the case in other fields, but it is almost guaranteed in public health.

Public health managers have a unique relationship within the communities they serve. They are expected to be both broad and deep subject-matter experts and effective public policy leaders and also be connected to local politics—an incredible amount to handle. As one of our local health directors stated, "People really do expect me to know about everything from how to control dog bites to the risk of avian flu."

Moreover, the public health enterprise is different from other organizations. In some ways, the differences are good. Most people get into public health work because they care about people and want to make a difference: this fills public health organizations with people with high ideals and goals, who are not necessarily driven by a "return on investment" motive. The perception of this quality can give a public health organization a reputation of being an "honest broker" in the community, trusted by political leaders, business colleagues, and other community members. However, all organizations need a "return on investment," however that is defined. Do you know your programs actually work? How much do they actually cost, and will you be able to sustain them over the long term? What if the grant runs out or government priorities change? These types of questions require idealistic public health professionals to think about "return on investment," and "sustainability," and even "revenue generation"—terms we ran away from the business world to escape.

Finally, everyone seems to have a stake in what public health organizations do: taxpayers, the public health "customer" (who is everyone, whether they know it or not), local and state politicians, the media, community competitors for some of the services offered, local employers, educators, businesses . . . the list goes on. How much any one of these stakeholders supports public health is closely tied to economic well-being, either personal or communal, to political whims, and to the perception of crisis. Public health organizations have to manage in economic downturns and changes in political priorities and communicate need and raise awareness without overdoing the "crisis" message. All of this is a lot to juggle.

How Do We Know the Subject?

Now, we do not pretend to know everything about public health practice. You will notice that none of us is a local public health department manager, for example. However, we have gleaned what we know from reliable sources: from our own education and experience managing our own enterprises in the public health, healthcare, and education fields; from our colleagues and clients at the North Carolina Institute for Public Health and at the Dana-Farber Cancer Institute; and from the hundreds of students who have come through the executive education and certificate education programs at the North Carolina Institute for Public Health for whom, in essence, we began writing the "Management Moment" in the first place. These include the over 1,000 graduates of the Management Academy for Public Health who have come in teams since 1999 to learn about applying business planning in their work. Our students also include the prominent leaders who have attended the Centers for Disease Control and Prevention–sponsored National Public Health Leadership Institute (PHLI), offered by the North Carolina Institute for Public Health in partnership with the

Public Health Institute of Oakland, California, and the Center for Creative Leadership in Greensboro, North Carolina; and finally, the students of our other leadership institutes, the Southeast Public Health Leadership Institute, the Emerging Leaders in Public Health program, our Certificate Education programs for working professionals, the Food Safety Leadership Institute, and the PREVENT (Preventing Violence through Education, Networking and Technological Assistance) program. These public health professionals have helped us know what challenges public health professionals are facing, what tools and resources they need, and where they want to go from here.

In a way, this book is a collection of "lessons learned," as managers and from managers, over the years. Here are some of those lessons:

1. PUBLIC HEALTH MANAGERS NEED GOOD "PEOPLE SKILLS."

Public health workers, like workers at any profession, expect more than a paycheck. And because in some cases public health workers are not getting very big paychecks, they may expect a lot more than a paycheck. This expectation may translate into a desire for mentoring and personal development opportunities, which need to be fully supported by their supervisors and organizational culture for them to be successful. Also, as the workforce ages and retires (a crisis in and of itself), the younger workers coming in are used to working in teams and thinking in terms of "group projects": they deserve well-planned and well-managed teams to facilitate their projects, and their manager needs to be able to handle (and welcome) diversity, recruit good colleagues, deal with difficult interpersonal situations, and maintain a satisfied workforce over the long term.

The first several chapters in this collection cover "managing people," offering concrete advice for building, motivating, and maintaining your own team. They look at ways to be more effective both personally and interpersonally, give hints on creating a positive work culture, and define what "diversity" can mean, and why it is important, to the contemporary manager.

2. PUBLIC HEALTH MANAGERS NEED TO UNDERSTAND THE WIDER COMMUNITY.

Maybe there never was a day when public health organizations were strictly isolated from nongovernmental realms of health care and other businesses, but if there was, it is over now. A lot of what the contemporary public health manager does is manage relationships with people outside the health department doors, developing and maintaining partnerships in an increasingly interdisciplinary field. The proliferation of possible partnerships for public health entities is good for generating ideas and strengthening broad support for public health programs. It is good for actually getting things done in the current economic and political climate. However, it does require skill and diplomacy, a dose of humility, and (always) a healthy sense of humor.

All the leadership programs that we have developed at the North Carolina Institute were founded as partnerships. We worked with the Kenan-Flagler Business School and the Center for Creative Leadership and School of Public Health departments, such as Epidemiology and Biostatistics, to bring the best resources possible to the table to meet the needs of our clients. Partnerships have been key to our success—and they will be key to yours.

The second set of chapters that follow provide examples and definitions of good partnerships: what makes good partnerships and how to build and maintain them, how to analyze stakeholders, and what is the difference between management and leadership in this regard.

3. PUBLIC HEALTH MANAGERS NEED TO BE GOOD COMMUNICATORS.

Public health has a lot of audiences. With new technologies come greater expectations for how quickly and broadly we can share information with the community. With the changing workforce, expectations are increasing for timely, transparent top-down communication within the organization. A manager has to know what can (and should) be communicated, and how. Good communication can translate into success at spreading health information, improving the image of the health department in the community, and positively affecting the political process. Bad communication can translate into misunderstanding or mistrust (within and outside of the public health organization), not to mention poor health outcomes.

The third set of chapters that follow cover how best to communicate with a variety of audiences, from successfully connecting with your colleagues of all levels, to managing with the myriad of new technologies available, to handling the nitty-gritty of effectively speaking, writing, and presenting your ideas.

4. PUBLIC HEALTH MANAGERS NEED TO UNDERSTAND THE BUSINESS OF RUNNING AN ORGANIZATION.

Most of the participants in the Management Academy come to us needing help reading the most basic financial spreadsheet; even those at the National Public Health Leadership Institute, who have been handling big budgets and complicated funding models for years, profess that they are not facile with finances. The need to understand fiscal management is ever growing. Why? Because the key competency for success in public health is the ability to get resources. And you have to understand finances to get sufficient resources to realize your dreams for your community. The final chapters of this book cover both basic and innovative fiscal management for public health managers: thinking creatively about sustainability, applying business thinking to public health challenges, and fundraising from corporate and private foundations.

This Is the Beginning

Again, most of these chapters were initially published as "Management Moment" columns: as the name implies, they are meant to succinctly address acute, concrete problems rather than systematic, long-term challenges of the public health system. We hope you will find them useful as you face the expected—and unexpected—challenges that you come across every day. If they spur questions and ideas for future columns, please write to us at thepublichealthenterprise@unc.edu. We'll be happy to hear from you.

Section **1**

Managing
People

Chapter 1

The Coach in You

Janet E. Porter and Edward L. Baker, Jr.

What is a public health leader's greatest knowledge or skills deficit? It seems most everyone has an opinion about the knowledge or skills that leaders need to acquire. In *Public Health: What It Is and How It Works*, Barney Turnock explained,

> Senior public health officials must have the preparation not only to manage a government agency, but also to provide guidance to the workforce with regard to health goals or priorities, interact with stakeholders and constituency groups, provide policy direction to a governing board and interact with other agencies at all levels of government whose actions and decisions affect the population whose health they are trying to assure.

Louis Rowitz outlined in *Public Health Leadership* the innumerable talents, traits, skills, and perspectives required to be the consummate public health leader. The Institute of Medicine identified in *The Future of the Public's Health* that leaders must have "expertise in their specific subject area; substantive expertise in the content and values of public health and competencies in the core skills of leadership . . . skills for vision, communication and implementation."

Chapter Source: © 2004 Wolters Kluwer Health | Lippincott Williams & Wilkins. Originally published in *J Public Health Management Practice*. 2004; 10(5): 472–474.

So, the skills, knowledge, and competencies required are known, but the question remains, how are current public health leaders performing in terms of the core skills? One way to answer this is to look at the 360-degree performance data collected for the 155 public health leaders who completed the National Public Health Leadership Institute (PHLI) between 2001 and 2004. Those PHLI scholars from across the United States had 1158 peers, superiors, subordinates, and clients complete the Center for Creative Leadership's (CCL) Benchmarks® assessment to evaluate their skills in meeting job challenges, leading people, and respecting self and others. The results over the three cohorts were remarkably consistent. For all three, the number one leadership deficit was in "confronting problem employees." You might say this is not a leadership skill; this is a basic management skill. And, you would be right. Being able to effectively address your team members who are not performing is a basic managerial skill that is needed just as much for entry-level managers as for health directors.

Leaders in public health will say they are rated poorly at confronting problem employees because they work within civil service systems, with unions, and with government bureaucracies that limit their flexibility. However, the 88,731 private-sector respondents who have evaluated their leaders with the CCL's Benchmarks instrument, also have identified "failure to confront problem employees" as the number one deficit for over 10,000 leaders who work in Fortune 500 companies, associations, not-for-profits, the military, and the government. Clearly, we in public health are not unique in not having the skills—or the incentives or support systems—to address problem employees.

Does this matter, you might ask? The largest Gallup poll ever conducted—over one million employees—tried to determine whether a relationship existed between the work environment and organization performance. In other words, does what employees think really matter in how well an organization performs?

Gallup's results were surprising, not because the answer was "yes" but because what really matters to employees in terms of staying in jobs and performing well was unexpected. Gallup determined that the strength of a workplace can be measured by employees' responses to questions such as, "Do I have a best friend at work?" "Is there someone at work who encourages my development?" or "Are my coworkers committed to doing quality work?" Human resource departments have traditionally focused on schedules, benefits, pay structure, and grievance procedures; yet, satisfaction or dissatisfaction with those job dimensions does not impact organizational performance as much as whether employees like their boss, their coworkers, and their team. As the saying goes, employees don't leave their job, they leave their boss. The Gallup research validates the importance of middle and senior managers in determining organizational effectiveness.

Great Managers Are Great Coaches

Because managers were determined to be critical to organizational performance, Gallup interviewed over 80,000 managers across 400 organizations to understand what the world's greatest managers do differently. They then summarized their findings in one word: fit. Yes, fit. Great managers have the innate ability to fit employees with the position or work that needs to be done. And, perhaps more importantly, to address those who are not a fit.

Who fits people to roles—positions—expertly? Coaches do. The job of a coach is to prepare others to dunk the basket, to land the puck, and to cross the goal line. The coach sits on the sidelines hoping he has selected the right players, put them in the right positions, prepared them for their respective positions, taught them how to play together—hoping they will score the most points and win the game. But the coach isn't the one who plays the game.

Herb Brooks, another in a long line of coaching legends whose story has been brought to the silver screen, was featured in the 2004 movie *Miracle*. Highlighting the relatively inexperienced U.S. Olympic hockey team's 1980 win over the dominant Soviet Union team, *Miracle* credits Brooks with the ability to select the right kids for the right positions and then to optimize their performance in those positions. In one of the movie's most powerful scenes, Brooks is being admonished because he is not selecting the best players, and he responds, "I'm not looking for the best players, I'm looking for the right players!"

So what does coaching have to do with confronting problem employees? The first question to ask yourself is how you would define your role. Several years ago, a senior leader who had just lost his job commented, "How can they do this to me? In the 15 years I have been here, there has never been a major mistake!" This leader defined his role as leadership = control. He saw the leader's job as controlling people, projects, and schedules. And, yes, it was true that there were no major mistakes during his tenure but neither was there innovation or partnering with other community organizations or staff development. What he most valued, what he brought to the organization, was risk-free management, which was not what the organization valued.

If you define yourself as a coach, then your number one job is to maximize the performance of those on your team. This is more important than program development, budgeting, or strategic planning. As another famous coach, Knute Rockne, said, "You win with the people!" If you see yourself first as a coach, it will have a powerful effect on how you spend your time. Coaches spend their time understanding what the team needs to get the job done, selecting the right person for every position, and then giving them instructions and feedback. And, when the coaching process fails, they recognize that it is not working and do something about it.

Assembling a Winning Team

So, back to this notion of fit. What is required for a coach to effectively fit the right person in the right position? First, the coach has to have a clear idea of what competencies are required for every position. Years ago, a group of managers were interviewing candidates for a director of nursing position. The interviewers, none of whom were nurses, could not begin to evaluate the candidates' nursing philosophy, conceptual framework, and skills currency. Often, candidates are hired based strictly upon whether people like them in the interview because the manager and the hiring staff have not invested sufficient time thinking about the expectations of the role and what skills the ideal candidate will bring. Coaches spend time really thinking about what is required in a position for the team to be successful.

Then coaches prepare players for their positions by teaching them their roles and introducing them to others players' roles. They help players practice their roles, debrief them on how they performed in the practice, and then help them practice again. How much time do you invest in teaching your employees' their roles and introducing them to others' roles? This can be time consuming, but you don't have to see yourself as the only coach on the team. Many organizations have a system of appointing "on-board" coaches to serve as peer coaches for new employees. This system has been employed by many organizations to support workforce diversity by providing a support system for underrepresented minorities.

During practice, the coach observes team performance, provides encouragement and feedback, and then takes notes. After practice, the team is debriefed on how they performed, and the coach commits what they have learned to writing and develops a game plan to improve. In *The Fifth Discipline: The Art and Practice of the Learning Organization*, Peter Senge identifies that learning organizations invest in reflecting on their performance and how to improve performance constantly. When was the last time you led your team through a debriefing of a major event or incident or even facilitated their reflection on their current performance? Just asking, "How do you think we are doing?" or "What could we do better?" at your next staff meeting can unleash a torrent of creative ideas about how the team might function more effectively.

When Coaching Fails

Even with fit, practicing, and debriefing, what do you do when the coaching fails? In public health, rather than getting the person off the team, we often move them to another position. And, as Gallup identified, great managers are skillful at moving employees to the right position because they see the hidden talent in the individual, not because the employee needs to be moved off the team. So, the first step is to ask whether this individual's talents can be better suited to another position. Jim Collins has extensively studied the characteristics of companies that have outstanding performance. As Collins asked, "What if you don't want them in another seat, you want them off the bus?" The coaching process with a problem employee begins with getting the employee to see that a problem exists (see Figure 1.1).

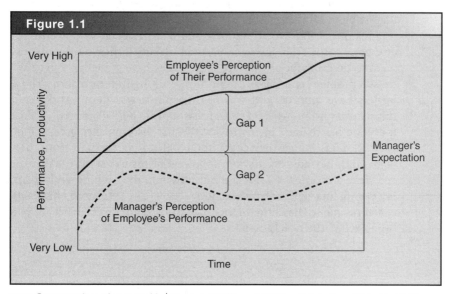

Figure 1.1

Source: © 2004 Wolters Kluwer Health | Lippincott Williams & Wilkins. Originally published in *J Public Health Management Practice.* 2004; 10(5): 472–474.

Convincing an employee that a problem exists is often difficult because the employee sees the performance gap (Gap 1) as all the tasks they are performing that are beyond minimal job expectations, whereas the manager sees the performance gap as the difference between a consistent standard of performance and the failure of the employee to meet even minimal standards (Gap 2). The first step in the process is for the manager to hear the employee describe his or her perception of his or her performance. It is quite possible that the employee will enlighten the manager about unheralded contributions he or she is making, but the manager needs to be prepared to provide specific examples that illustrate Gap 2. The manager needs to understand why the employee is failing to perform and to work with the employee to develop alternative solutions. Then, an action plan for correcting the performance with clean expectations about performance needs to be developed. For example, the manager needs to reach an agreement with the perpetually tardy employee that 8:00 a.m. is the starting time and that the frequency of the employee's arrival by 8:00 a.m. will be observed for the next month. The manager and employee need to agree to meet again to evaluate performance relative to the agreed upon standard.

Confront the Employee and Strengthen the Team

The PHLI program incorporates coaching sessions on "Confronting the Problem Employee" because the message from the scholars' colleagues of the need to strengthen this skill has been so powerful. In every one of the coaching sessions, public health leaders have come forward to describe the arduous processes they have gone through to address a problem employee, oftentimes resulting in termination. These leaders have reported, "It was so difficult. It was the most difficult thing I ever did in my career. But it has transformed my team." Almost everyone has made a hiring mistake. What distinguishes great public health leaders is that they coach their staff to get the best from their team, and they address it when someone needs to get off the team.

Take a moment to think about how you're coaching your team. Do you define your role as coaching? How can you more effectively coach people so they fit with their positions? And, finally, what are you doing when the coaching fails?

Chapter 2

Management Is a Team Sport

Janet E. Porter and Edward L. Baker, Jr.

Most public health staff can relate to the thought recently expressed by Nancy Cripps, a program assistant at the North Carolina Institute for Public Health (NCIPH). Reflecting on the joy of working with her neighborhood association, she exclaimed, "Just when I was about to give up, everything turned around. All of a sudden, we just have such a good team! It seems like there isn't anything we cannot do. And I'm not even sure why." A gratifying team is like what's been said of obscenity. You're not sure you can define it, but you know it when you see it.

Do you remember when you were a part of a great team effort and how incredibly satisfying that was? It may have been years ago, and it may have been a community-wide effort or just a small team in the public health agency that came together to tackle a specific task. Oftentimes, the best team efforts are born from crisis—having to do the impossible with no resources and no time. Every start-up company founded by dream-weavers with unending stamina has tales about getting the product out the door, and the adrenaline rush that came from that wave of success. What energy is generated from people feeding off of each other's sense of possibilities! We all look back with great fondness at the sense of brotherhood that came from not having just survived—but thrived—by overcoming insurmountable obstacles and accomplishing

Chapter Source: © 2004 Wolters Kluwer Health | Lippincott Williams & Wilkins. Originally published in *J Public Health Management Practice.* 2004; 10(6): 564–566.

the impossible. Legends are born of efforts that live on in every not-for-profit company and government agency in America.

Despite Nancy's exclamation that she wasn't sure what essential ingredients created a great team with monumental results, if you listened to her description of the transformation in her neighborhood, all the elements are there.

Team Ingredients: Diversity, Respect, and Empowerment

> We really draw upon the strength and talents that our diverse community has to offer. After one member started a garden club, a single mother started a knitting circle, and the next thing you know another family had started a bible study.

Powerful messages: diversity, respect for talents, empowerment. Of course, because public health is an amalgam of disparate disciplines—environmental health, nursing, nutrition, epidemiology—glued together by a common mission of improving community health, we think we know the value of diversity. But really embracing diversity means actively thinking about how each new hire will broaden the perspective of the team and challenge their thinking. It is a paradigm shift for a manager to transition from thinking about hiring for each position, not in terms of who the best candidate is for that job but in terms of what type of person will most benefit the team.

To respect the talents of others, every member of the team has to appreciate that each person's role is equally important. Years ago, while running a workshop to challenge staff to think about creating a vision for their future, a receptionist stood up to present her pictures that illustrated the team. One of her three pictures was of machinery with interlocking cogs and wheels—all different sizes but obviously interdependent. She simply stated, "We need to operate like a well-oiled machine. Like all machines, some parts are bigger than others, but all are equally important, for even if the smallest cog breaks, the machine stops. And, the oil that lubricates our working parts, is the love we have for each other and for the communities we serve." You could hear a pin drop in that room and some eyes welled up as they looked at the little hearts she had drawn between the cogs to represent love. With her hand-drawn picture, she had so eloquently described that everyone was equally important to the overall functioning of the team regardless of how seemingly insignificant their tasks. This team was so in love with that drawing that they had it blown up, mounted and framed, and hung at the entrance to remind everyone who walked into that unit that they all mattered to get the job done.

Empowerment is fundamentally about trust. Gene, the NASA commander portrayed by Ed Harris in *Apollo* 13, has the unenviable task throughout the film of solving one mounting crisis after another in an attempt to get the Apollo 13 astronauts home safely. At one point, when CO_2 is fatally rising in the crippled space capsule, Gene directs a team of engineers to "figure out how to fit a square air filter in a round hole." Now picture this: the engineers go and do it without any interference from Gene. Even though the eyes of hundreds of millions of people throughout the world were watching NASA's every move, Gene trusted those engineers to solve the problem. Empowerment requires trust. If you don't trust your team, you need to step back and ask whether it is an issue of skills, unclear roles, poor working relationships, or lack of tolerance for failure.

Welcome New Members to the Team

> The welcoming committee greets every new family and tells them they have moved into the best community in Durham. Then we talk about the community activities and the friendliness of the neighborhood.

Most organizations realize the powerful socialization process that happens during employee orientation. Psychologists have long known of the power of primacy and recency. We remember our first encounter— and our most recent encounter. People remember their first day at work, who asked them to lunch, having to ask to be taught basic tasks like using the copier, or their first staff meeting. What happens in those first hours or days at work is a powerful socialization to the code of conduct in the workplace. Nancy's welcoming committee creates expectations about the way neighbors will treat neighbors, about the way neighbors will take pride in their community. Do you have an organized employee orientation? Does your orientation reflect the core values of your public health agency, or is it basically about policies and procedures? If it is the latter, then the message new staff get is that rules matter more than knowing the names of other staff or serving the community.

Individuals Make Up a Team

Of course, we also have an annual neighborhood association meeting where we talk about what we want to accomplish in the next year and how we might work together to accomplish those goals.

Disparate people doing disparate tasks are unified by common goals. Teams become teams rather than individuals when they work together to accomplish something larger than any one could accomplish alone. In leadership development courses, one of the most powerful exercises is for a group to go through a ropes course. One of the most challenging exercises for the University of North Carolina leadership groups is called the spider web. In this exercise, the entire team is on one of side of a web of roping strung between two poles—similar to a widely strung volleyball net. The team has to figure out how to get everyone to the other side of the "net" by having members step through the various holes without touching the net or using any of the holes more than once. The teams have to strategize, make decisions, and work together to be successful. Some teams will spend hours trying to figure this out—even though there is no concrete reward. Successfully accomplishing the task is reward enough. Does your team have an overarching goal that everyone can see is a part of what they do each day?

Often, the problem with annual goals and objectives is that they are not simple, meaningful, or visible to the majority of the staff. One group of staff held a "What We Would Be Proud Of" workshop at which the group identified what would make them proud if it were accomplished in the next year. Then the list was made into a big poster, hung on the wall, and everyone walked by it every day. If an item was accomplished, one member of the team got to ceremoniously strike that item off the list. "Done!" To bond a team, goals accomplishment needs to be visible.

True success in reaching team goals is when no one remembers which parts of the project or the goal belong or are attributed to a particular person. The project is owned by the whole. A few years ago, a team at the North Carolina Institute for Public Health designed a team-building exercise called the "museum walk" for a leadership program. In this exercise, teams must illustrate their team project without using words. The exercise tests artistic ability, but it also challenges teams to portray the most essential parts of their project for others. When this exercise was first conducted with great success, NCIPH team members were elated with the outcome, and they all attributed authorship to one another. As a result, they could not remember who originated the idea.

Communication Keeps the Team Together

One reason everyone in our association knows what is going on is because we use every avenue for communication.

Teamwork requires communication. Coaches have long meetings with their basketball, football, or soccer teams to communicate each team member's assignment with split-second precision. Ann Bancroft, the noted South Pole explorer, describes in the video made about her all-women, cross-country skiing expedition, *The Vision of Teams*, that one of the most important aspects of their teamwork was working out an effective method of communication, despite glaring ice and temperatures below -40° Fahrenheit, while swaddled in winter wear. She states that ultimately they decided as a team that acknowledging each other—even with a grunt or a pat—was essential as they skied past one another to switch off on who would take the lead and face the howling winds. Whether it is through complicated hand signals that are indecipherable to anyone but the pitcher and catcher or a company newsletter, deliberately designing a communication plan that says "we" to the team is essential to bonding between individuals.

Employee satisfaction surveys invariably point out that communication could be better. As one human resources director stated, "Employee satisfaction surveys that say communication should be improved are the bane of my existence." One of the major mistakes managers make in trying to improve communication is telling more "what" and not enough "why." Staff—like vital team members—want to know not only what they have to do but also why they have to do it. How does their role fit into the big picture? It is easy to feel insignificant until someone communicates how vital your part is to the overall team. One example is to think about how an entire murder mystery can be ruined if the butler fails to point out the letter opener missing from the desk in the drawing room—a line which all other actors are using as their cue.

Learn from Team Mistakes

> We also have learned from our mistakes. Not all of our clubs and events have been big successes, but we have learned from them to do better the next time.

Learning organizations—and learning teams—improve because they learn from their mistakes. And mistakes are tolerated—even encouraged—as long as the team debriefs, reflects on lessons learned, and does better the next time. *The Vision of Teams* portrays Ann Brancroft's South Pole team practicing and failing, learning from their mistakes, practicing and failing, learning from their mistakes. One key element of learning organizations is debriefing sessions that are held after every major event to review the logistics, the processes, the outcomes, and to provide constructive feedback between the teammates to improve performance the next time. In debriefings, the coach is merely the facilitator ensuring a systematic, nonthreatening review of the event supporting feedback between teammates, not necessarily even needing to provide feedback himself.

Memorable teams not only work well together and get things done, but also want to work together again because of the positive experience. Unfortunately, teams often reach their goals but never want to work together again. Years ago, an Ohio team of physicians and administrators spent almost two years meeting each week to structure a contractual relationship between the parties. They succeeded in striking a deal but ultimately failed because they were so sick of one another they didn't work together on anything for the next two years.

Leadership Makes the Difference

> It was speed bumps and lighting, both of which had been tried before to no avail, which ultimately made all the difference in this neighborhood. And that would not have happened without leadership.

Virtual teams emerge in work settings to get goals accomplished, dissolve, and sometimes leave an indelible impression on the organization's future. Yet, even those virtual teams have someone in an informal leadership role who helped to connect the dots, to keep the group on schedule, to provide a sense of energy. Leadership does make the difference in teams.

Summary

We have discussed several key principles that build teams. Good communication will keep the team focused. Make sure team members understand the big picture and keep communicating along the way; celebrate successes, analyze failures, give your teammate a pat as you ski the trail. Appreciation for diversity will enhance your team and give it a much broader base of skills to draw on. Empowering team members builds individual confidence and spills over to the rest of the team; give team members permission to take on new projects without micromanaging. Finally, recognizing your team members' talents helps create a whole larger than the sum of the parts; some parts may be bigger than others, but all are equally important.

Chapter 3

Creating Public Health Management Teams That Work

Kimberley Freire, Rebecca Davis, Karl Umble, and Anne J. Menkens

Coming together is a beginning.
Keeping together is progress.
Working together is success.

—Henry Ford

Public health has always required multidisciplinary collaboration. In recent years, the field has redefined how public health professionals should collaborate and who should be included. For example, the Institute of Medicine has called on public health leaders to collaborate with private industry, media, health care, academia, and government.[1] The National Institutes of Health's "roadmap" states that "research teams of the future" must be multidisciplinary and involve public and private alliances to spur innovation and accelerate the translation of science to practice.[2] More broadly, the global "New Public Management" movement, known as "reinventing government" in the United States, calls for agencies to decentralize and partner to develop creative solutions to health and social problems.[2–4]

So, public health managers have to link up with new partners. But how can managers actually form collaborative teams that improve public health work?

Chapter Source: © 2008 Wolters Kluwer Health | Lippincott Williams & Wilkins. Originally published in J *Public Health Management Practice.* 2008; 14(1): 76–79.

Frank LaFasto and Carl Larson, who have studied thousands of teams in a variety of organizations, define *teams* as "a special type of collaborative group that forms to create or change something specific."[5] Teams are built to act. This makes them different from task forces or boards that are formed only to advise or support an effort. Furthermore, collaborative teams rely on joint decision making and peer leadership and may not have a single leader with executive authority.[5,6] Team members, therefore, need to be able to work together to accomplish specific tasks. Because health programs can stand or fall, depending on how well teams work together, developing competent teams has become a priority in health management and leadership training.

Offered by the School of Public Health and the Kenan-Flagler Business School at the University of North Carolina at Chapel Hill, the Management Academy for Public Health is a leadership and management training program that has worked with teams of public health managers and community partners for almost a decade.[7] The hallmark of the Management Academy is its focus on team and project-based learning. Teams learn skills in managing people, money, and data. To practice the skills and to develop innovative strategies, each team develops a business plan for a health program within its community or state. Nonprofit business experts and academy faculty coach teams through business plan development and implementation.[8]

Recently, we interviewed representatives from 40 teams who attended the academy during 2003–2005. We asked them what factors are most important to accomplishing team goals, in this case implementing their business plans. Many of their conclusions echoed LaFasto and Larson. We have selected the top five themes to present here, along with some suggestions for how you, as a manager, could try to implement their advice.

Team Members Must Commit to a Common Goal

The first task of the team is to articulate and agree on what they are trying to achieve. As one manager put it, "You all need to know where you're going and what you're doing." Articulating a common goal is as much about the process as it is the end point. Some respondents explained that reaching a common goal meant that all team members had input and "bought in" to their overall business plan concept.

How can you keep the team goal-oriented? There is nothing like writing things down to get them moving forward. Get your team members to hash out exactly what their expectations are, to identify and agree on the primary goals, to write them down, and to all sign the document. In our office, we print out the list and make it into a poster, laminate it, and mount it on the wall of our meeting room. At the end of the time frame for the project, we put stars next to the goals that have been met, add new goals, or carry over those that need further work. Logic models are another excellent tool for building consensus and mutual understanding of what the team is trying to achieve—and how progress can be measured.[9]

Team Members Must Commit to Doing the Work

When team members "buy in" to the project goal, they are likely more motivated to execute project tasks than when they concede to a majority or unilateral decision. As one respondent explained, "All people on the team need to be passionate about the plan, otherwise you'll run out of steam halfway through." This seems particularly important for teams with few members and those operating without a solid organizational structure to provide support and team replacements. Good teams quickly identify members who are not able or willing to see tasks through: the "weakest links" can drag on team members' motivation and progress toward their goal. But when they see all members contributing, they draw on the energy and stay focused.

How can you build commitment? Think about drawing many people into your decision-making process, so you are not just dumping work on people's desks. Once a project is under way, find out who needs and wants more direction from you, and step in to help. At the same time, give more freedom to those who want to work more independently. If you identify a weak link, work with that person to identify how he or she can contribute to the program or what problems he or she is experiencing that are not being expressed. Strong social ties also help; we will put forth a lot of effort to help our colleagues when we are also friends in the journey. So team leaders should build the bonds among team members—over meals or coffee, through going to a ball game— to forge stronger commitment. If you make your team into a caring "family," it will be easier to address conflicts or misunderstandings when they emerge. Strong teams must trust one another's commitment and intentions, as well as one another's wisdom and skills.

Teams Should Build on Their Members' Strengths

Management Academy strengthens management and leadership skills. As managers' skills grow, our research shows, so does their confidence. Some team members, however, are good at managing people, while others are more comfortable—and effective—with money or data. "Don't try to make creative people into accountants," one participant told us, a sentiment echoed by many. Identify team members' strengths and "nonstrengths," identify leaders, and set people up to succeed at their assigned tasks.

How can you identify and build on strengths? Many individual development instruments help identify individuals' strengths and preferences with regard to work style, personality traits that affect work, and strengths to build on. Team-building experts often work such instruments into their activities, for the benefit of both the manager's and individuals' own understanding of their strengths and weaknesses. Use your team members' annual evaluations to talk about what they like best to do, what you perceive they are best at, and think about ways you can help them be more effective at all of their tasks. If you do not use the instruments, start off team projects with an open discussion of who is good at what, how each member likes to work, and how the team will function. That can help the team get off on the right foot. Many teams find "team charters" to be a great tool.[10]

Team Leaders Must Facilitate Effective Communication

Collaborative leadership is driven by consensus instead of executive decision making. That means communication is essential. Some of our participants believe that the team leaders' major role is to facilitate communication so that the team can reach agreement on actions. Team leaders should seek input from all team members and encourage dialogue among members, especially when problems or conflicts arise. In fact, several participants expressed that "healthy conflict can be a dialogue," and managing conflict through productive discussions was key to progressing in plan implementation. With respect to leaders and communication, one manager explained: "The leader needs to have the skill to manage the team . . . to encourage [the person who is introverted] to give ideas and concepts and make sure that the person that tends to dominate the conversation is held to a minimum—in a kind and tactful manner so that one person does not dominate the entire plan." Communication is important to bringing together people with different personalities, work styles, and perspectives to work toward a common goal.

How can you facilitate better communication? Do not be afraid to bring up or deal openly with conflicts or other difficult issues. Without pointing fingers or putting anyone on the spot, try to air things that seem to be holding up work. Leaders may need to apologize for oversights or mistakes—and thereby to set the tone for humility and problem solving on the team. Be sure also to communicate when things are going well: hold up good examples of teamwork and accomplishments; give "awards" that show you are recognizing the hard work the team is putting in. At the end of a period of hard work, our team often has a meeting in which specific accomplishments are named and kudos are generously given—supplemented with gourmet ice cream bars!

Balance Team Member Diversity and Common Interests

Team diversity is important to accomplishing project goals. Many participants talked about how different skills, perspectives, and interests made their team stronger. In particular, teams need expertise in finance and data management, program development, and community outreach. Some participants, however, found that common interests with teammates helped build their relationships. For example, one team consisted of epidemiologists from different health districts. This team found their common backgrounds helped them discuss project issues and empathize with their teammates.

How can you build diverse teams that work well? If you have a role in the hiring process in your organization, you may be able to build your staff with the teams in mind. Hire people with good team skills, in addition to technical competence. Hiring people who "fit" with the values of the team and organization, and who work well on teams, will help programs flourish. Those kinds of people are also likely to stay longer in your shop. In your dealings with the community, local business people and other healthcare professionals try to forge connections with people who will bring a different perspective to your teams. You may have to educate people about what public health is and does, how public health affects many other realms of society, and why they should care about (and become partners with) public health practice. In sum, finding people with different perspectives and interests can help your team, as long as the interests are not extremely divergent and as long as they know how to work well on a team.

As organizations move toward a new management style that emphasizes collaboration and innovation, competent teamwork is very important. In our study, managers shared their advice on what managers and supervisors should consider when developing teams within their organizations, as well as when they link across professional fields and sectors. Focusing on team goal development, emphasizing project buy-in while clearly defining individual tasks and goals, identifying and using individual strengths, and allowing for teams to be made up of members with variable skill sets while building on common interests or backgrounds are all key components to successful team development. We recognize, and our own research shows, that a large part of what makes a team successful is external to the team: the organizations, communities, and other outside interests have substantial influence on what teams can accomplish. A good start, however, is to build a team that has the best potential to work.

References

1.   Institute of Medicine. *The Future of the Public's Health in the 21st Century.* Washington, DC: National Academies Press; 2003.

2.   Office of Portfolio Analysis and Strategic Initiatives, National Institutes of Health. National Institutes of Health roadmap. Available at: http://nihroadmap.nih.gov. Accessed August 29, 2007.

3.   Kettl D. *The Global Public Management Revolution: A Report on the Transformation of Governance.* Washington, DC: Brookings Institution; 2000.

4.   Osborne D, Gaebler T. *Reinventing Government: How the Entrepreneurial Spirit Is Transforming the Public Sector.* New York, NY: Penguin; 1992.

5.   Lafasto F, Larson C. *When Teams Work Best: 6,000 Team Members and Leaders Tell What It Takes to Succeed.* Thousand Oaks, CA: Sage; 2001.

6.   Crislip D, Larson C. *Collaborative Leadership: How Citizens and Civic Leaders Can Make a Difference.* San Francisco, CA: Jossey-Bass; 1994.

7.   Orton S, Umble KE, Rosen B, McIver J, Menkens AJ. Management Academy for Public Health: program design and critical success factors. *J Public Health Manage Pract.* 2006;12(5):409–418. This issue is devoted to the Management Academy for Public Health.

8.   Orton S, Menkens A, Porter J. *Public Health Business Planning: A Practical Guide.* Boston, MA: Jones and Bartlett, 2009.

9.   Program Development and Evaluation, University of Wisconsin–Extension. Logic model. Available at: http://www.uwex.edu/ces/pdande/evaluation/evallogicmodel.html. Accessed September 18, 2007.

10. Team Charters: getting your teams off to a great start. Available at: http://www.mindtools.com/pages/article/newTMM95.htm. Accessed September 19, 2007.

Chapter 4

The Behavioral Event Interview: Avoiding Interviewing Pitfalls When Hiring

Claudia S. Plaisted Fernandez

One of the hardest tasks a manager faces is building a successful team. In fact, difficulty selecting and building a team is one of the top three predictors of future derailment, according to research by the Center for Creative Leadership (CCL).[1-3] Hiring the wrong person for a job is a common experience. In my own seminars, classes, and coaching, I get many a knowing nod when I ask whether participants have "hired a person for their technical skills . . . and then found that the whole person showed up for work!" Mistakes in hiring can create serious interpersonal issues among staff members and headaches for managers and leaders. Hiring is often considered a tricky and dangerous business, particularly in civil service systems where correcting a hiring mistake is a lengthy and costly process. The job turnover created by poor person–job fit also presents wasted expenses to organizations in both the public and private sector.

A common way a manager builds a team is through interviewing candidates and hiring. However, building a real team that thinks for itself while executing the organization's mission in creative, innovative, and agile ways is more challenging than a manager might suspect.

As LaFasto and Larson say in *When Teams Work Best*, "a successful team begins with the right people"[4(p.xxviii)]. However, getting the right people to the table presents a serious challenge. The right people must

---

Chapter Source: © 2006 Wolters Kluwer Health | Lippincott Williams & Wilkins. Originally published in *J Public Health Management Practice.* 2006; 12(6): 590–593.

have more than technical skills. Although technical skills, which constitute a working knowledge of the job tasks at hand, are critical, equally important are the "soft skills" that characterize the make-it-or-break-it team dynamics that ultimately govern team productivity, innovation, and agility.

Interviewing Errors to Avoid

Five problems typically plague the old standard interviewing style common in today's workforce (see Table 4.1). The first error a manager makes when hiring is to spend most of the interview talking about the position or the organization. What the interviewer should be doing is listening intently. Unfortunately, what often happens is that candidates receive a lot of information about the job, but the organization knows little about the candidate beyond the resume.

Archaic and uninformative interview questions present a second common problem with the interview process. "What are your strengths and weaknesses?" is a weak tool to understand either the soft or hard skills a potential hire has to offer. Candidates often have much-practiced and uninsightful information to share in response to such an inquiry.

A third common error is in how interviewees are asked to talk about their relevant work experience. Typically, candidates are asked to describe their experiences in specific jobs. Candidates have an opportunity to describe themselves at their best and to tell their interviewer choice stories, providing a verbal presentation of their resume. However, there is no guarantee that these stories will shed light on how they would perform on tasks relevant to the currently open position.

Table 4.1
Five Common Interview Errors
1. Talking more about the job than about the candidate
2. Asking for strengths and weaknesses
3. Getting a verbal resume
4. Asking hypothetical interview questions
5. Hiring for chemistry rather than fit

Source: © 2006 Wolters Kluwer Health | Lippincott Williams & Wilkins. Originally published in *J Public Health Management Practice*. 2006; 12(6): 590–593.

Furthermore, without a good deal of follow-up questioning you might never know what important facts or events might have been omitted.

A fourth, less serious, interviewing error is to present a scenario to a candidate and ask, "What would you do in this situation?" While it does assess some technical skills (e.g., does the candidate know the correct procedure, the correct medication dosage, the correct paperwork to complete), it does not assess whether the person actually follows his or her own advice in a real-life situation. Book knowledge does not always predict behavior. Answering an abstract "what if" question allows the interviewee to present an ideal scenario with his or her impeccable behavior at the center of the story. It makes for a good interview from the candidate's perspective, but it has relatively less predictive value for how the candidate will actually perform in the job, particularly if the question revolves around interpersonal aspects of work rather than dry, technical, fact-based tasks.

However, the most serious error a manager can make in hiring is to hire for chemistry—that sense of how you click with a candidate. Do not make the error of thinking that chemistry describes a hiring preference or a criterion because the failure to hire well is one of the top reasons that managers derail, according to research from the CCL. In hiring for chemistry, the manager often ends up with a like-minded team that mirrors his or her own weaknesses. While having good chemistry (interpersonal workings) within the team can be helpful and constructive, "going on one's gut feeling" should not be the guiding factor in making a new hire. There are many steps a manager can take to promote the chemistry and cooperation of the team after the players with the best fit are chosen. These steps will be addressed in other chapters in this book.

"Don't hire for chemistry" does not imply that you should ignore the candidate's people skills, often called "soft skills." These skills are critically important to nearly every job in public health and certainly to positions in management and leadership. The difference is this: feeling the chemistry in interviewing describes a potential colleague who you would like on your team, who seems to have a similar worldview to yours, who might make a good golf or lunch partner, who you can conceive of becoming a friend. That might be great icing on the organizational cake, but it does not measure a candidate's soft skills, hard skills, or organizational fit. In fact, one of the most valuable assets a leader can have is a team that represents a diversity of worldviews, maybe even differences in perspective, which would make a lunch out not quite so, well, appetizing. Fit is not about "fitting the leader's preferences." It is about finding the edge that the organization needs.

Past Performance Predicts Future Success

So what is a manager to do? Professional human resource firms and headhunting agencies have figured this one out: the first step is to throw out the old style of interviewing candidates. Rather than ask prospective employees, "What are your strengths and weaknesses?" or "What would you do?" when presenting various work-related scenarios, instead it is critical for the manager to find out how the candidate actually performed in the past. Past behavior predicts future behavior. If you interview candidates regularly, a good mantra to put on your wall is *in human behavior, the past predicts the future.* Choose the candidate who has proved himself or herself in the past on tasks relevant to those required for the position.

Corporate and academic recruiters call this technique the Behavioral Event Interview (BEI). The BEI is a way of interviewing that demonstrates effectiveness based on actual experience. In *Competence at Work*, Spencer and Spencer wonderfully describe how to conduct this process.[5] Development Dimensions International has a patented version of the process called Targeted Selection (see www.ddiworld.com). The first step in this BEI process is to examine the job description (see Table 4.2). Pull out the critical areas that will determine the success of the person in this position and fashion open-ended questions about how the candidate has accomplished similar tasks. For example, if partnering and leading collaborative efforts are critical to successful job performance, then prepare a question that elicits how the interviewee managed the interpersonal and creative aspects of partnering and collaborating. By asking the candidate to describe a time when she had to create partnerships with another organization or group despite contentious relationships between the parties, you will gain insight into several dimensions of

Table 4.2
The Steps of Behavioral Event Interviewing
1. List the critical performance areas for the job.
2. Create open-ended questions that query the candidate's experience at those tasks.
3. Gather data on the Situation, Task, Action, and Result (STAR) in the candidate's answer.
4. Evaluate the answers for demonstrated job performance.
5. Compare their answers to other candidates' answers (this is sometimes done with a point system).

Source: © 2006 Wolters Kluwer Health | Lippincott Williams & Wilkins. Originally published in J *Public Health Management Practice.* 2006; 12(6): 590–593.

behavior, such as innovation, creativity, and the ability to get along with others and create win-win opportunities.

Steps to Successful Hiring

Let us examine this a bit more closely with a public health example.

Step 1. List the critical areas of job performance, which, for a U.S. Air Force epidemiologist, includes the following:[6]

- Conducts preventive medicine and communicable disease control, occupational health, food safety, and disaster response programs.
- Applies epidemiological and statistical methods to identify and evaluate factors increasing disease morbidity and mortality.

Step 2. Craft questions to ascertain the candidate's actual behaviors in relevant situations, such as

Tell me about a specific experience you had conducting a disaster response initiative. Specifically, I'd like to hear how you addressed the communicable disease issues that arose from the incident.

or

Tell me about a time when you applied statistical methods to identify and evaluate factors relating to disease morbidity and mortality. I'd like to hear about how you translated that information into policy recommendations.

Step 3. Listen very carefully—and take copious notes to record the situations candidates describe, the tasks they had to accomplish, actions they took, and the results they achieved. This is called the STAR method, or Situation, Task, Action, and Result. It is the interviewer's guide to conducting a successful, informative interview. You can use it to quickly scan the candidate's answer for missing information and continue to probe. Some helpful probing questions include "Who was present?" "What were you thinking or feeling at the time?" "What happened as a result?" "What was your role?" "What did you say?" and "What did you do?" These follow-up questions will help you examine the depths and relevance of the candidate's experience.

Step 4. Judge how well candidates answered the questions and how their answer demonstrates their skills. You could even create a 5- or

10-point-value scale for how well their experience matches your needs and assign the points earned to each answer. Discussing the STAR answers given and the point values assigned with colleagues who also used BEI to interview the candidate will help you gain expertise in this method.

Step 5. Compare the different job candidates' BEI results with your colleagues to ascertain who has the experience and skills that fit your organization.

Let us look at another, less tangible, example. Organizational culture is a critical factor affecting the productivity of a team, an office, or an organization. Leaders and managers can have a great impact on organizational culture. As Janet Porter and Edward Baker say in Chapter 1, "employees don't leave their job, they leave their boss." It is imperative for managers to hire individuals who will create a positive, constructive culture within their organizations. How can you ascertain what new hires might do to affect this often-troublesome area? Ask them to tell you about a time when they had to take steps to change or influence the culture of their organization.

When using BEI, look out for generalizations such as "well I usually . . ." or "typically I. . . ." If the candidate offers a general response, then you need to ask, "Can you give me a specific example?" Also, be sensitive to the interviewee's theorizing about how he or she would respond, and again follow up with specific questions about the actual experience. Some candidates unfamiliar with BEI might at first be unnerved by this questioning, but with your patient follow-up probing, they should be able to share their relevant experience with you. Similarly, if they have difficulty answering, their lack of experience will also be abundantly clear.

Your next step is to decide whether they have the skills to do the job. Certainly, not everyone will need to have experienced every aspect of a job to be able to perform well. We all remember when we got our first position supervising or managing others or had major budgeting responsibility for the first time. As managers, we know there is a first time for everything as one progresses through one's career. Look for evidence that the candidate is coachable and has taken opportunities to grow, to receive feedback, to improve on skills, and to develop talents. Self-reflection, identifying developmental areas, and successfully addressing them is a significant meta-skill. This is especially true of soft skills. A senior leader I coach once said something that is true of most senior-level managers and leaders: "I know I'm a smart person. I know I can learn the technical skills of this new area. I've learned a lot in my life—that's not the hard part. It's the people issues that present the real challenges." You can use BEI to identify difficult-to-assess skill areas that make or break organizational and team success. You can also use these techniques to help safeguard yourself from the most common errors in hiring.

Professional human resources firms and headhunting agencies typically use the BEI process. Their follow-up questions are carefully crafted, and points are awarded for answers so that each interview can be compared. Even without going to such lengths, the technique as outlined can help you make the right hiring decision the first time and lower employee turnover costs to your organization.

As you use the BEI techniques, you will build a team that should have highly predictable performance and interpersonal interactions. Because past behavior predicts future behavior and past performance predicts future performance, you should find few surprises in how your team meets challenges, collaborates, and innovates.

References

1. Lombardo MM, McCauley CD. *The Dynamics of Management Derailment*. Greensboro, NC: Center for Creative Leadership; 1988. Technical Report No. 34.

2. Wacyk C. Diagnosing and addressing leaders derailment—the role of the executive coach. Available at: www.nelsonconsulting.co.uk/Articles/exec-coach. Accessed August 30, 2006.

3. McCall MW Jr, Lombardo MM. *Off the Track: Why and How Successful Executives Get Derailed*. Greensboro, NC: Center for Creative Leadership; 1983. Technical Report No. 21.

4. LaFasto F, Larson C. *When Teams Work Best*. Thousand Oaks, CA: Sage; 2001.

5. Spencer LM, Spencer SM. *Competence at Work: Models for Superior Performance*. New York: John Wiley & Sons; 1993.

6. U.S. Military. U.S. Military Air Force Officer job descriptions. 43HX Public Health. Available at: http://usmilitary.about.com/library/milinfo/afoffjobs/bl43hx.htm. Accessed August 30, 2006.

Chapter 5

Employee Engagement

Claudia S. Plaisted Fernandez

It is every manager's dream to lead a team of highly engaged workers. High engagement means higher productivity. It means higher morale. It means *mission critical* becomes *mission accomplished*. Just how engaged does the workforce of this new millennium look? And more important, what can a public health manager do to help employees become more engaged and more successful at work?

In 2003, one of the largest management and human resource consulting and administration firms, Towers Perrin, conducted a study of workforce engagement.[1] Querying 40,000 workers, they found that American and Canadian workers share a very strong work ethic. Fully 78% of these workers say that they are personally motivated to help their company succeed and are willing to put in the extra effort required to make that happen. Seventy-seven percent stated that they really care about the future of their company and 70% said that they are proud to work there. Most (61%) felt their company is a good place to work. So the research showed that workers feel the "good will" of their companies. Good will matters because research shows that it is the foundation for true engagement, and engagement is strongly related to higher performance and productivity. That productivity matters underscores the reality that *people matter*.

Chapter Source: © 2007 Wolters Kluwer Health | Lippincott Williams & Wilkins. Originally published in J *Public Health Management Practice.* 2007; 13(5): 524–526.

Don't Mistake Employee Satisfaction for Engagement

Are you thinking, "I know my employees are all satisfied in their jobs"? Think again. Employee *satisfaction* is not the same as employee *engagement*. According to the 2005 Walker Loyalty Report,[2] satisfied employees pay only lip service to their company commitment. While a whopping 80% report that they like the duties and activities that make up their jobs, the report shows that they may jump ship tomorrow for a job with slightly more pay or a better benefits package. The Walker Loyalty Report classifies workers into four categories: (1) loyal—who have a personal attachment to your organization; (2) accessible—who go the extra mile but intend to leave; (3) trapped—who want to move on but feel they cannot; and (4) high risk—who are ready to go. Nearly 60% of the surveyed workforce fell into the latter two categories. Truly loyal employees are priceless: 95% said they go "above and beyond" the call of duty, while just 62% of those lacking loyalty do the same.

Because managers cannot rely on employee satisfaction to help retain the best and the brightest, employee engagement becomes a critical concept. The Towers Perrin report found that 17% of employees are "highly engaged," the bulk of employees (64%) are moderately engaged, and 19% are disengaged. That nearly one of five employees may be "marking time" should concern any manager. Not surprisingly, non-profit-sector employees are far more engaged than their industry peers—42% fell into the highly engaged category. How do these folks maintain this level of commitment? It appears to reflect their personal sense of mission and passion. The take-home message: a personal connection to work is fundamental to building employee engagement.

How to Promote Engagement

So, how do you manage people to promote engagement? The challenge at the low end of the engagement spectrum is to identify these disengaged folks and determine how to reengage them. Disengaged employees feel their contributions are being overlooked; they concentrate on tasks rather than on outcomes, and they want to be told what to do. They do not have productive relationships with their managers or with their coworkers. According to *The Leadership Advantage*, "managers who only provide tasks to an employee reinforce *not-engaged* behaviors and actually move 180 degrees away from engaging the heart, mind, and soul of that person."[3]

People become disenchanted at work for many reasons, such as interpersonal issues or a negative organizational culture. It is essential to build good relationships with these employees and regularly communicate expectations, clarification, and measurement. Reframe the position description from completing tasks to achieving goals and outcomes. Good questions to ask employees include "What are the outcomes you are supposed to achieve? What were you hired to do? How do you contribute to making this a great place to work?"[3] Focus your disengaged employees on outcomes as well as on the steps it takes to get there. Using *measurement* is crucial to an employee's feeling of success, as long as what you are measuring is outcome-oriented.

Managers would do well to nurture engaged employees because these workers produce more and contribute to good working environments in which people are productive, ethical, and accountable. In the corporate world, they make more money for the company and create emotional engagement and loyal customers. They stay with the organization longer and are more committed to quality and growth than are *not-engaged* and *actively disengaged* workers. Engaged employees do all this through their relationships with others. They tend to have strong relationships with managers as well as clear communications with them, are focused on a clear path on the basis of their strengths, and enjoy strong relationships with their coworkers. These relationships create the foundation for them to take risks and to stretch for excellence. Do not leave these excellent employees alone. For best results, spend most of your time with the most productive and talented people because they have the most potential.[3]

Of course, the big question is how to move that 64% in the middle up to the highly engaged status—and how to keep them there. The risk is that they will slide down toward the disengaged group, and that could severely affect your organization's performance. Most employees are just waiting for management to take the right steps to make them fully engaged. When employees move from moderate to high engagement, they are almost twice as likely to want to stay with their job and give the extra effort required to get the job done, and done well.

Retain Employees, Invest in Their Skills

The flip side of employee engagement and retention is turnover, that financially crushing cost center that plagues many organizations. Turnover is expensive, slows productivity while new employees "learn the job," and costs you organizational memory. Engagement and turnover have a strong relationship: the Towers Perrin study showed that only 6% of the highly engaged are out hunting for their "dream job," but 11% of the moderately engaged and a whopping 29% of the disengaged are job hunting. Although at first it might seem acceptable to have the disengaged jump ship, they are generally far more costly to replace than they are to motivate. And, don't forget: some of those disengaged job seekers could be in key areas in your organization.

So, what is it that attracts, and then engages, good employees? Your first thought might be "money," but that is only part of the story. According to the Walker Loyalty Report, the factors that *attract*, *retain*, and *engage* employees can be divided into four categories: (1) pay, (2) benefits, (3) learning and development, and (4) work environment.[2] When it comes to attracting employees to your organization in the first place, benefits, pay, and "work-life balance" are the important factors. Learning and development plays a lesser role, with "career advancement opportunities" coming farther down the list of important factors for workers surveyed.

When it comes to keeping those employees (employee retention), surprisingly neither pay nor benefits makes it to the top five factors chosen. The category of learning and development looms large when it comes to retention, with "career advancement opportunities," "retention of high-caliber people," and "development of the employee's skills" ranking high on the list. Work environment plays a strong role, with "overall work environment" and "resources to get the job done" both ranking in the top five of important factors.

With regard to employee engagement, pay and benefits do not even make the top ten! All the factors fall into the categories of work environment and learning and development. The most important factor for employee engagement is "senior management's interest in the employee's well being," followed by "having challenging work," "decision-making authority," "customer orientation," "career advancement opportunities," "company reputation," "collaboration with coworkers," "resources to get the job done," "input into decision making," and "senior management vision."

Although pay and benefits are key to recruiting people, they actually play a far lesser role in retaining and truly engaging employees. That is good news to the typical public health manager. In public health, we usually cannot reward our employees financially as well as we could in the private sector. However, managers can do several things to get the other aspects of the workplace right: providing development opportunities, good supervision, effective performance management and communication, and clarity about how employees contribute to results. If you want to keep workers around, use this as a checklist of things to work on in your own management style and organizational culture development.

References

1. Working today: understanding what drives employee engagement. Available at: http://www.towersperrin.com/tp/getwebcache doc?webc=HRS/USA/2003/200309/Talent 2003.pdf; http://www.keepem.com/doc files/Towers Perrin Talent 2003(TheFinal).pdf; http://www.keepem.com/doc files/Towers Perrin Talent 2003%28TheFinal%29.pdf. Accessed May 9, 2007.
2. Walker Loyalty Report, November 2005. Available at: http://www.walkerinfo.com/what/loyaltyreports/studies/employee05/factsheet.cfm. Accessed May 9, 2007.
3. The Leadership Advantage. The power of employee engagement. http://www.leadershipadvantage.com/employee Engagement.shtml. Accessed May 9, 2007.

Chapter 6

Managing a Diverse Workforce: The Manager's Impact

Robert C. Amelio

R ecently, a public health manager attending the Management Academy for Public Health* was hurt by the feedback she received from her staff during her 360-degree assessment. They rated her poorly in terms of managing diversity. She thought she was doing a good of job of being inclusive in hiring and in promoting a diverse workforce. However, rather than ignore this feedback, she was proactive about going back to her health department and making diversity an agenda item at a staff meeting. She told them she was surprised that they did not think she embraced diversity and wanted to understand more from them about what she should be doing. This statement led to a rich conversation about how she was not helping them deal with the challenges of serving a diverse population in their county. They commented that they felt unprepared and needed more coaching and resources from her so that they could better do their jobs to meet the needs of the ever more diverse population in their county.

A recent review of management seminars focusing on diversity include titles such as How Managers Can Enhance Diversity, Valuing and Honoring Diversity, Understanding Diversity, Managing Diversity, Appreciating Diversity, and Managing Diversity Internally to Help Others Externally.

---

*A yearlong training program in business skills for public health managers, run by the North Carolina Institute for Public Health and the University of North Carolina Kenan-Flagler Business School.

An organization that embraces diversity is an inclusive organization. Inclusiveness means that different types of staff and customers feel welcome and comfortable; that staff are judged on their merits and their contributions rather than whether they "fit in"; and that people feel that they are treated fairly regardless of their age, religion, ethnic origin, disability, gender, or sexual preference. Can you say that your health department is inclusive?

Managers are expected to do many things with diversity: enhance it, value it, honor it, and understand it. What's a manager to do to know what "diversity in the workplace" really means and how his or her behavior affects diversity? How does the public health manager begin to make sense of this vast world known as diversity in the workplace?

Diversity: The Macro Level

Diversity should be viewed from the macro, or systems, level, as well as the micro, or individual level. At the organizational, or macro, level, diversity comprises those policies and practices of an organization that include or exclude members of the workforce or that have a negative or positive effect on the workforce. Such things as hiring and promotion practices, salary increases, how bonuses are awarded, office or lab location are all examples of diversity on the organizational, or systems, level. Other examples that may not be as obvious include the paintings and pictures on walls, the food served in the cafeteria, who speaks and is listened to at meetings, or who is invited to lunch with senior managers.

Diversity: The Micro Level

At the individual level, diversity refers more to differences among members of the organization and how each of us responds to and effectively works with these differences. A good example of diversity at the individual level involves the multigenerational workforce: a worker in her sixties versus one in his twenties. While the younger worker might have greater understanding of the latest technology, the older worker might have a better grasp of how to work with the organization's bureaucracy. Instead of working against his employees' differences, a manager who is truly committed to diversity will see these differences as strengths each individual brings to the organizational mission. At the same time, the committed manager will see past this type of stereotype: it is not *necessarily* true that older workers are technologically inexperienced or, more importantly, unable to learn new things. Such perceptions can be detrimental to good working relationships. For example, at a recent diversity seminar in an academic healthcare organization, a female staff member in her early seventies admitted to lying about her age to a new manager, a woman in her thirties, so the new manager would not assume she could not learn new technology. From experience, the older woman had learned to expect some prejudice against her age, but her own assumptions about the younger woman were also telling. A "diversity mature" manager, that is, one who understands the value of differences among staff members, will encourage cross training and communication that help different individuals teach and learn from one another.

A Model of Diversity

Many models of diversity are used to help workers and managers conceptualize diversity more concretely. One extremely useful model of diversity is The Four Layers of Diversity (see Figure 6.1).

This model can help the manager understand that diversity comprises many characteristics of people at work, not only a few. The diversity-mature manager will seek to understand these factors and dimensions of diversity to ensure he is bringing out all aspects of an individual's talents and abilities to support the organization's mission and goals.

The Four Layers of Diversity

The first layer, personality, includes an individual's likes and dislikes, values, and beliefs. Personality is shaped early in life and is influenced by, and influences, the other three layers throughout one's lifetime and career choices.

The second layer, internal dimensions, includes those aspects of diversity over which we have no control (though "physical ability" can change over time because of choices we make to be active or inactive or because of illness or accidents). This is the layer in which many divisions between and among people exist and which forms the core of many diversity efforts. These dimensions include characteristics we first see in other people, such as race, gender, or age, and on which we make assumptions and judgments.

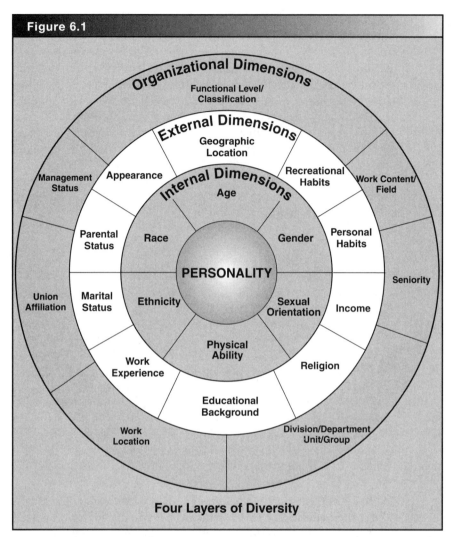

Figure 6.1

Four Layers of Diversity

Source: Reprinted with permission from *Diverse Teams at Work*, Gardenswartz & Rowe (2nd Edition, Society for Human Resource Management, 2003).

The third layer represents external dimensions, aspects of our lives over which we have some control, that might change over time, and that usually form the basis for decisions on careers and work styles. This layer often determines, in part, with whom we develop friendships, and what we do for work. This layer also tells us with whom we like to associate, and decisions we make in hiring and promotions at work.

Finally, organizational dimensions represent the culture found in a work setting. Preferential treatment and opportunities for development or promotion are affected by the aspects of this final layer.

This model describes the dimensions that shape and affect both the individual and the organization. The "internal dimensions" often receive primary attention in successful diversity initiatives; however, the elements of the "external" and "organizational" dimensions often determine the way people are treated, who "fits" or not in a department, who gets the opportunity for development or promotions, and who gets recognized. A manager who wants to understand diversity and be an effective manager of a diverse team needs to pay attention to all these layers of diversity with the goals of using both differences and similarities to enrich the work environment and to bring the organization closer to its mission.

Some "Four Layers" Exercises

The Four Layers of Diversity is not only a useful model, but it can also be used as a teaching tool. To develop your own understanding of the effect of diversity on your life, try using the four layers as a reflective tool:

1. Read over the factors on the four layers. Think about how the various factors influenced the choices and decisions you made up to this point in your career. Which have had a positive impact? Which have had a negative impact? Which are you proud of? Which do you try to hide from others, if any?

2. Looking at the factors again, think about those factors you have difficulty accepting in other people. Which factors cause you to make snap judgments? Which influence your decisions at work in a negative manner? What factors cause you to try to avoid contact with others?

3. To explore your values as a manager, create a list of your staff members. Next to each person's name, write some of the factors from the dimensions that you are aware of and those you assume to be true about the person. For example, Jason: white, middle class, college degree, single, Catholic. You can select different factors for each person. Then ask yourself, How do I treat this person differently, both in a positive and a negative manner, based on what I know, or the assumptions I am making, about the person? Where are my biases coming out?

4. Finally, the four layers can be used as a team-building exercise by having staff members work through Exercises 1 and 2 individually, and then discussing their responses together.

The Manager's Effect on Diversity

Let us look closely at the effect you can have on diversity. Research has shown that people tend to leave their jobs because of poor management at the individual level rather than because of discontent with the entire organization. Therefore, each manager has a prime responsibility to create an atmosphere that seeks out, encourages, and praises diversity in all its dimensions. Diversity is more than just hiring people who are different from you and others into the workplace. The real commitment to diversity comes when the manager works hard to include all opinions, ideas, and styles of staff into the success of the organization.

Management Behaviors for a Positive Impact on Diversity

Many lists could be created on effective management behavior, gleaned from the hundreds of management books and conferences that abound. The following are some of the most important behaviors managers need to recognize and develop in a public health setting:

1. Understand that diversity encompasses many dimensions of being human, not only the internal dimension.
2. Do your homework on yourself. Develop your own awareness of your biases and hot button issues and how these come out at work. We all have them. A truly effective manager knows what makes her angry and who he gravitates toward in hiring, and is willing to change unproductive behavior.
3. Stretch yourself. Put yourself in situations that take you out of your comfort zone. Attend meetings and conferences that focus on people different from yourself: if you are a white man, attend career fairs targeting diverse workers. If you are a PhD researcher, take time to have lunch with administrative staff members and ask them questions about themselves.
4. Ask questions and then listen. This is one of the most difficult behaviors for many managers. We tend to learn unconsciously

that once we become managers we have the answers and need to tell others what to do all the time. Individual growth and inclusion of others rarely comes from talking. We learn about others by asking questions and then listening.

5. Accept that you are a role model 100% of the time. Staff members watch who managers laugh with, what jokes they tell, the language they use, who they go to lunch with, and who they send to conferences. In the workplace, the manager is always "on."

6. Encourage time to discuss process, not just content. Ask staff members questions, such as "What am I doing that helps you do your best work?" "What am I doing that prevents you from doing your best work?"

7. Read. Look for articles or books on subjects such as class differences, race, or gender identity.

8. Assess your management of staff meetings. Do you call on everyone who wants to speak? How do you respond to comments of lower-level staff members as opposed to those who are more senior? Let everyone have a turn at leading staff meetings.

9. Stand up for others. When you hear someone berate others publicly, especially a manager at your own level or someone you manage, follow up with that person and state your concerns about this behavior.

10. Reflect on your recruitment and hiring practices. Are you actively seeking new staff from throughout your community? What factors determined your most recent hiring or promoting decision? Have you created an inclusive environment?

Diversity requires work. It requires having conversations that don't feel comfortable. A few years ago, the University of North Carolina at Chapel Hill selected *Blood Done Sign My Name*, by Timothy B. Tyson, as their freshman reading assignment, the book all first-year students must read before coming to campus. At the invocation that year, Tyson spoke to students about the reading group discussions they would be having the next day about the book, which is focused on race. Explaining that we tend to pull back, to be careful with our words when we discuss uncomfortable topics, he admonished students that the only way they would learn about their own attitudes about race and stretch themselves was to "lean into it"—to unflinchingly face the issues raised in the book. He went on to say that "leaning into it" is exactly what they should do throughout their college careers. Otherwise, they would not really get the broadening experience college had to offer.

The greater the diversity among workers, the more likely misunderstanding or tension will occur. A diverse-mature manager knows how to have crucial conversations that push people past their comfort zone, that stretch them to understand their own biases and how that affects the way they work with others. When diversifying your workforce along any of the dimensions discussed, actively acknowledge differences, build your team, and help your staff members learn to value one another's strengths and differences.

Chapter 7

The Power of Positive Personal Regard

Claudia S. Plaisted Fernandez

In the corporate world, job titles confer power: positional power. You do what the vice president says because she is the VP; you do what the chief says because he is the chief. In the corporate sector, managers have other tools with which to motivate and reward their team as well. Money options include salary increases, promotions, stock options, and bonuses, whereas nonmonetary rewards include office space, leading a team of direct reports or support personnel, greater visibility, and tangible things such as company cars. Those are some mighty attractive "carrots." Demotions, salary cuts, removal of privileges, loss of bonus, and even dismissal make up the dark side of the tool set. Of course, the "stick" can also be applied as a motivational tool. It is fairly easy to lead and motivate a team with either a carrot or a stick.

However, not every manager has such attractive carrots—or harsh punishments—to give out. Some fields have few carrots and few sticks. As for titles, often in public health our titles fail to convey what we do and fall far short of symbolizing any "power of the office." What is one to do with pockets empty of such tools? In the public realm, being an effective manager means working with different tools. None can be more effective than personal power.

Chapter Source: © 2007 Wolters Kluwer Health | Lippincott Williams & Wilkins. Originally published in *J Public Health Management Practice.* 2007; 13(3): 321–323.

Public health managers can use *personal power* to be effective leaders. Think of a brick building. Bricks are important. They make up the external structure; they are tough and durable, but it is not the bricks that hold the whole thing together: it is the mortar that keeps the bricks in place and the whole building from collapsing. The bricks are the people in an organization. The mortar is the *positive personal regard* that keeps the organizational bricks there and working together to achieve common goals. Positive personal regard combines how we treat and speak to one another, how we appreciate the contributions made, and how we respect one another's role in the organization. It includes how we listen to each other with intent and meaning and how our own personal behaviors are worthy of respect as well. Positive personal regard in the workplace means that we honestly respect our colleagues and believe in their genuineness, even if we might disagree with them about the best course of action to take.

A manager can take several steps to develop better positive personal regard. These can be put into three broad areas: *inclusion*, *control*, and *appreciation*. Research led by William Shutz[1] has provided a good understanding of how people are fundamentally oriented to interpersonal relationships.[2,3] Let us explore inclusion, control, and appreciation to see what you can do to make your organizations stronger through mortar, not bricks.

Inclusion

Most people work in public health because they care about serving others. Inclusion is feeling like you belong to something larger than yourself. It is about being involved. For many, inclusion is participating, being recognized, feeling distinct, and knowing your contribution makes a difference. As a manager, you can do many things to inculcate a feeling of inclusion in your colleagues.

To send nonverbal signals that your team is significant, listen attentively, make eye contact with them, acknowledge their presence and successes, introduce them at meetings, acknowledge their participation, and create opportunities for people to participate. For some, inclusion is having a sense of prestige in what they do and in the respect others give them. Managers who fundamentally feel their colleagues are significant "show up with ears" (i.e., they listen) and integrate everyone into the discussion because they feel their contributions are important. Inclusion can be a powerful motivator. When workers feel significant in the office, they are much more likely to give that extra 10% that makes everyone else's jobs easier. Workers who understand their importance to the mission do not leave until the job is done and done well.

Control

Two types of *control* issues motivate workers. Some *want* control: they are motivated by power, authority, influence, and responsibility. A manager has to assess whether he or she can mete out responsibility and authority as a part of job growth, and do so, if appropriate. Many employees are highly motivated when they hear their boss say, "It's your show, you're in charge" because it feels good—it feels *competent*—to be in control, and, in general, people are motivated by feeling competent. Certainly, they are unmotivated when they are made to feel incompetent.[4] This motivation exists even if one is in charge of relatively small decisions. Deciding what color their office is painted, for example, can go far in helping people to feel in control of their daily destiny at work. Delegating effectively is an important skill that many managers find difficult.

Workers also appreciate a type of control exerted by "the boss." Even if the opportunities to mete out responsibility are few, many people are motivated by working with someone who, in addition to being fair, honors deadlines, keeps meetings focused, and remains mindful of time limits. Working with a supervisor who offers structure, gently directs actions, and suggests closure is what many workers respect and need to get their jobs done efficiently. However, managers who are chronically late or unorganized, let meetings run overtime, and are not mindful of deadlines tend to diminish the motivation of their subordinates.

Appreciation

Affection, or appreciation, is the most powerful motivating factor of the three. In offices, this is how we express support, encouragement, or appreciation for others. When we say, "I liked your report," applaud their presentation, or even ask about a colleague's weekend, we are sending a message beyond the context of the job: we are saying that we appreciate them. It sends a deep message about their worth to us and to the organization and speaks to the "organizational family." Organizations have many ways to give an "organizational hug" to employees. Employee of the Month is a common way to recognize individuals. At the North Carolina Institute for Public Health, we have a much-coveted parking spot next to the front door that used to be assigned to the director but is now reserved for an exemplary employee of the month. Some of us have plaques of appreciation or awards on our office walls. Our marketing team does a nice job of noting accomplishments in IMPACT, a newsletter, complete with photos of our team members. Go one step farther: contact your local newspaper or televised news program to run a story about your best and brightest in their "good news" section. A wonderful way to highlight your staff is to publicize their accomplishments to the community.

Appreciation is important because people tend to leave jobs when they lose the emotional connection to the work they do and with whom they work, not because of money.[5,6] Finding ways to creatively and sincerely thank employees—to acknowledge that they are not cogs in the organizational wheel—is not just good manners, it is good management.

Other actions a manager can take to show appreciation include mediating conflicts, identifying the energy and resistance levels in the group, helping the group to feel supported, and providing feedback.[7] These activities send the message that your team means enough to you that you will work for their mutual harmony.

Of course, in public health, we do not simply work with our own teams. We also must work with our community partners—often groups of stakeholders over whom we have absolutely no authority or control. Understanding what motivates people, what they care about, why they do what they do can be a big asset of personal power for a public health manager who must convene these diverse groups and lead them to consensus and partnership. Getting our own team, community partners, legislative stakeholders, and community members to the table with ears and eyes open and hearts and minds present can be difficult. Often the most important tool in our arsenal is positive personal regard. It is the mortar for a strong public health system and for healthier communities.

References

1. Shutz WC. FIRO: A Three-Dimensional Theory of Interpersonal Behavior. New York: Holt Rinehart & Winston; 1958.
2. Hammer AL, Schnell ER. The FIRO-B Technical Guide. Palo Alto, CA: Consulting Psychologists Press; 2000.

3.   Waterman JA, Rogers J. *Introduction to the FIRO-B Instrument*. Palo Alto, CA: Consulting Psychologists Press; 2004.

4.   Weiner B. Attribution theory, achievement motivation, and the educational process. *Rev Educ Res*. 1972;42(2):203–215.

5.   Caver K. Workforce engagement: what it takes to create an engaged workforce. Presented at: Proceedings of the Southeast Public Health Leadership Institute program scholars; April 28, 2005; Chapel Hill, NC.

6.   Development Dimensions International. Data from the 2003 Towers Perrin Talent Report. Available at:http://www.towersperrin.com/tp/getwebcachedoc? webc=hrs/usa/2003/200309/talent_2003.pdf. Accessed October 23, 2006.

7.   Shell ER. *Participating in Teams: Using Your FIRO-B Results to Improve Interpersonal Effectiveness*. Palo Alto, CA: Consulting Psychologists Press; 2000.

Chapter 8

Promoting a Civil Workplace

Darlene Lewis

C ivility is often described as the opposite of incivility, which is like defining peace as the opposite of war or health as the opposite of sickness. Similarly, a peaceful workplace might be described as a workplace that lacks discord. Of course, a truly peaceful workplace, a workplace that can be more broadly defined as having a "culture of peace," does lack discord, but it has a lot more: it is a positive, desirable, attainable state that allows for the best work to be done. Peace does not mean that there are no disagreements. Rather, a peaceful culture means that the culture promotes civic harmony and that staff feel comfortable addressing disagreements rather than avoiding them.

As a manager, you have the responsibility, and the ability, to create and support a consistent culture of peace within your organization. You can do this by promoting peace, engaging others in the process, and transforming your organization through training and education.

The Manager as a Promoter of Peace

The United Nations named the 2000 decade as the International Decade for a Culture of Peace. They defined a culture of peace as a "set of values, attitudes, modes of behavior and ways of life that reject violence and prevent conflicts by tackling their root causes to solve problems through dialogue and negotiation among individuals, groups and nations."[1] Unfortunately, the goal of even a Year of Peace, much less

51

a Decade of Peace, has not been fulfilled on the international, national, or local level. However, the idea of a promoter of peace, one who "tackles the root problems," is important. When Nelson Mandela and the South Africa Truth and Reconciliation Commission investigated the human rights violations under apartheid, they looked at the role civil society played in maintaining the apartheid system. They concluded that even though the sectors of civil society, including the healthcare system, the judiciary, faith communities, the media, and business, may have acted within the laws of the country, their actions of commission and omission made them complicit in maintaining a "culture of human rights abuses."[2] In other words, they were called to task for not acting as peace promoters: they did not "tackle" the roots of the problem. To be a responsible person, the Truth and Reconciliation Commission suggested, is not just to refrain from doing evil but also to actively and consciously work for change and peace. Similarly, a manager must actively cultivate a culture of peace within the organization. Unless you actively work to change and improve the culture, you are reinforcing the status quo.

To be a peace promoter, first conduct a critical analysis of the workplace and the people within it, as they exist today. Start with yourself. In analyzing yourself, think about what's getting in the way of your creating a culture of peace workplace. What gifts do you bring that you can share? What tools and resources do you need to be more effective? How do you resolve conflict? Are you open to new ideas? Do you seek out different opinions and encourage staff to brainstorm different ideas? How did you address the most recent apparent conflict within your organization?

In your analysis of the workplace, think about some of the following questions:

- Are off-color jokes, which could be insulting to a particular group, common? Are prejudices against those who are different expressed in other ways?
- Is power used in inappropriate ways among employees or between management and staff? Is fear a common motivator?
- Is the leadership of your organization fair and transparent in their practices? Or, is there a perception of secrecy, or corruption?
- Do you sense that staff feel exploited?
- Is there a habit of gossip, complaining, or criticism in the organization, without positive ways to express this discontent?

- Are there individuals who seem so disgruntled or unbalanced that they may even undertake acts of violence against others?
- How are conflicts handled? Do you have resources for staff to help them resolve conflicts?
- Does staff feel free to constructively address issues when they believe they are being treated inappropriately, disrespectfully, or aggressively?

Some of these questions will be immediately apparent, while others are difficult to answer. Work to answer them by being open without judgment to the concerns of your staff. Although the questions are meant to get at organizational culture, they each describe individual actions. All of us are implicated in the dominant culture, the culture of maintaining the status quo, usually without even being aware of it. But with some understanding of the issues involved, we can all play roles in advancing a culture of peace.

Sometimes employee opinion surveys—especially qualitative remarks in response to targeted questions—will elicit the degree of incivility in a public health department or other organization. Some organizations use other surveys, such as the Denison Culture Survey, to unravel the strength and opportunities in building a stronger culture.

After you have gauged the level of incivility in your workplace, dedicate your work to moving away from the culture of incivility and toward a culture of peace and civility, characterized by core values, attitudes, and behaviors that indicate respect and intercultural understanding. Some characteristics of this culture would include respect for and tolerance of others, coexisting in harmony by listening to others and promoting solidarity, appreciating how different individuals contribute to the community, and ensuring democratic participation and equality for all within the organization.

The transition from a culture of incivility to a culture of peace requires individual, collective, and institutional transformation. Some things you might do to make this transition include the following:

- Empower staff at all levels with skills of dialogue, mediation, and peace building.
- Provide opportunities for meaningful participation of staff, including equal and diverse representation of staff in decision making at all levels.
- Allow for the free flow of information and transparency and accountability.

▪ As possible, eliminate inequalities of pay.

▪ Promote training and development for all.

▪ Advance understanding, tolerance, and respect for all staff through your own actions and the standards to which you hold others in the organization.

Implementing these changes can go a long way toward increasing morale and dedication to the organization in your employees.

Engage Others in the Process

Your job in creating a culture of peace is to encourage your employees to become more aware of what it means to be part of a diverse workforce and how individual actions can create or destroy a culture of peace within the workplace. Regarding yourself first, make sure to explicitly name the work you are doing as peace promotion work and truly question what you do to sustain the culture and what you can do to change it. Then you are ready to involve others in the quest by talking to them and encouraging them to become active and empowered as well.

Who should be involved? Ironically, if there are disrupters in your workplace, they may be the first people you want to engage in the peace-making process. It may seem paradoxical, but the most effective promoters of peace are often those who were most implicated in the culture of discord and disruption. Often, those who become involved in internal strife are convinced that the organization should be better. Their call for change can be seen as a commitment to the organization. Your job is to transform that desire for change into positive cooperative action.

Persons responsible for other types of discord, such as discriminatory or harassing behavior, require a different tack, but they can still be valuable peace promoters. They may need to be educated about and sensitized to the damage they cause by their actions. Sometimes it may be necessary to educate them about the law in regard to workplace civility. They may develop a clearer understanding of the forces driving people to harass or to discriminate against others and may be better able to confront them and prevent further discord. With the right consciousness, commitment, and training and education, if necessary, any individual or group can become a peace promoter.

We also know that informal leaders play a powerful role in shaping the culture. They serve as role models for others' acceptable or unacceptable behavior. So, know who the positive role models are and hold them up as exemplars in front of others. It is important that employees viewed positively in the organization who model civil behavior are recognized and appreciated.

Finally, consider those individuals who are not participating in explicit acts of conflict but who up to now have done nothing to confront them. They need to be sensitized to their role as "enablers," whose acts of omission are allowing the culture of incivility to exist. Do they speak up when the offensive joke is told? Do they act out of fear or help spread a culture of fear to others? Would they rather ignore the problems that face their organization than help to solve them? These are people you as a manager need to engage in your cause to bring openness and tolerance to your organization.

A culture of peace calls for nonconfrontational relations between individuals and work groups. Although it does not deny that conflict arises from diversity, it demands diplomatic solutions and promotes the transformation of destructive competition into cooperation on shared goals, through a process of healing and reconciliation.

The Role of Training in Creating and Maintaining a Culture of Peace

Undertake formal human resources training to build the culture of peace in the organization, for example, by holding group discussions and activities around issue of trust, prejudice, and sensitivity to others. As a manager, you should facilitate such trainings to maintain a safe atmosphere for expressing opinions and ideas, but you should not dictate the direction of discussion or exploration. Such trainings, if undertaken systematically and regularly, can help build mutual trust improve interpersonal communications, and, eventually, change attitudes.

Much training should focus on the first-line supervisors because they are the eyes and ears of public health organizations. They know how to spot problems at the earliest stages, and once trained, they can take action to deal appropriately with any situation. Lower-level employees would also benefit from such training because it gives everyone a chance to voice their concerns and frustrations and often diffuses the source of conflict before it causes problems. Studies show that ongoing training is most effective.

Unfortunately, incivility can sometimes escalate into actual violence in a workplace. To avoid such extremes, an organization must to include the following factors in its education and training:

■ Orient all employees to an unequivocal policy against all forms of violence.

■ Share clearly defined rules of conduct.

■ Teach managers pre-employment screening, supervision, and retention, focused on recognizing warning signs and threats.

■ Establish a competency model and provide management training specifically on violence prevention.

■ Have a defined mechanism for reporting violent or threatening behavior.

■ Give managers the authority to take immediate action against those who have threatened or committed acts of violence.

Consequences of Not Addressing a Problem

The basic consequence of not addressing incivility in the workplace is that you can create a workforce of low morale and a low level of loyalty or job commitment. In addition, lack of training may expose the organization to harassment lawsuits, negligence, or, in extreme cases, wrongful injury or death. Hundreds of thousands of dollars are spent settling such lawsuits, and millions are paid out when an employer is found to be negligent. Organizations that have been diligent about training may mitigate some of the damages by demonstrating to the court that they acted with due diligence and in good faith by educating employees on how to recognize and deal with the threat against them.

Fortunately, most incivility in the workplace does not rise to the level of violence against others. It just makes the workplace unwelcoming; the danger is that people will spend more time complaining than working. Turning that culture around is an important part of reaching your organization's goals and mission.

References

1.   U.N. Resolutions 52-13 and 53-243. Available at: www3.unesco.org/iycp/kits/res52-13_en.htm. Accessed September 17, 2008.

2.   *Truth and Reconciliation Commission of South Africa Report.* Released March 21, 2003. Available at: http://www.info.gov.za/otherdocs/2003/trc/. Accessed September 17, 2008.

Chapter 9

Making the Most of Your Time

Amy Porter-Tacoronte

Things which matter the most must never be at the mercy of things which matter least.

—Goethe

The most strategic and effective people are not managers of time, but of themselves, other people, and work. They have long accepted that trying to beat a clock, which is bound to keep ticking, is pointless. Instead, effective managers identify and focus on activities with the highest potential return. They have learned and consistently apply proven tools and techniques for organizing and managing tasks. Specifically, they are usually highly skilled in time sense, goal setting, time planning, and—most important—recognizing procrastination. If you use these skills well, you will be able to function strategically and effectively, even under the pressure of the modern public health department.

Time Sense

Time sense is estimating how long it takes to accomplish a task. It is an important skill for creating reasonable time frames and staying on track. For example, my husband's rough estimates of time are always way, way off. He is chronically late. Either he overestimates the time left to cook the pasta or he underestimates the time required to make it to the airport. In short, my husband has a poor sense of time. As a result, I've spent the past 20 years eating over- or undercooked foods and wishing I'd called a cab to take me home after a flight. Some people are better able to judge the passing of time than others, but fortunately, you can develop time sense by doing certain exercises. For example, practice guessing the time and checking it against a clock or with a friend with a watch (then keeping track of the difference). Another is to keep close track of how long projects actually take, and refer to that record rather than guessing the next time you plan a project. Or, as a last resort, listen to colleagues (or spouses) who tell you you're always late! An editor friend of mine always underestimated how long it would take to edit an article. Finally, she decided she'd take the time she guessed and double it, no matter what. That way, she can surprise clients by being early and not disappoint them by being late. Ultimately, by developing your time sense, you will have a greater self-awareness of how you currently use time. This will enhance your ability to recognize when you are falling behind and correct it. Imagine no more missed deadlines!

Goal Setting

Goal setting is another critical skill that will help you establish priorities, get organized, make important decisions, and stay on track. However, the goals must meet certain criteria. First, goals must be written statements that are specific and actionable. What are you going to *do*? For example, perhaps your long-range aim is to establish a program that enrolls local citizens in a county-run preventive health program. That seems specific and would involve some specific tasks, such as researching need, getting buy-in from local physicians, and so on. Another goal might be to delegate more to others. This is more vague, so you might want to identify which tasks you should delegate to which colleagues. Second, the goals should be measurable—if you can't measure it, then you can't manage it. If you're specific in your goal, then this part is easy: how many tasks can you delegate, or how many physicians do you need on your planning committee, or by what date do you want to begin serving customers?

Third, to manage them, you must make certain that the goals on your list are realistic. Never accept or promise what you can't deliver, and only accept or set realistic time frames, and then add a cushion. In short, a goal statement should describe exactly what you are striving for and the necessary steps for getting you there. With these elements, a skillful goal setter will have no problem building an action plan.

Time Planning

Time planning is the process of outlining in advance what work needs to be done within a specific time frame to reach the goals on your list. The ability to identify the activities and steps that are most important to do first is an essential step in time planning. Focus on these critical activities will help you work smarter, not harder. Many people spend their time running around like chickens with their heads cut off because they are not focusing on the right things. Most likely, their minds are cluttered—filled with an unorganized list of things to do. Effective time managers take the time to plan.

During a particularly stressful time at work (budget season), a friend was having a hard time sleeping. I suggested that she keep a pen and notebook by her bed at night and jot down everything she was thinking before she went to sleep—it worked! Writing helped to clear her mind and reduce her stress. This process works well at work also, but you have to take it a couple of steps further. First, write down all the tasks that need to be completed for a project—get it out of your head and into a trusted, reliable system that allows you to organize tasks in a logical, consistent way. Second, make sure that you are creating an action list and not just a to-do list. With a to-do list, you have to decide on the next action for each item, every time. However, with an action list, the next action is already determined; you simply have to choose which action to do. Here's an example. An action list might look like this: (1) call travel agent for quote, (2) establish budget, (3) buy tickets. This list has clearly defined outcomes and steps that allow us to focus on the next action. Say you want to establish a flu shot program at elementary schools. An action list might include (1) research staff and supplies needed for school-aged population, (2) compare cost of a mobile unit versus using space in the health department, (3) establish budget; and so on. An action list releases the mind to focus on getting the next step completed. Alternatively, a to-do list may read like this: (1) plan trip, (2) prepare presentation, and (3) cure world hunger. This list represents brain clutter with no defined next steps. It serves to muddle the mind and hold our attention while we struggle to define it. In short, without action lists, you may be perceived as dizzy, unfocused, and unreliable.

After establishing your action list, take one step at a time. If you have a large project, cut it into bite-sized, accomplishable tasks. This will prevent you from procrastinating and feeling overwhelmed. By listing all those tasks on a definite time schedule, you have converted your goals into a plan of action.

So what happens if, despite all your planning, you still fall behind schedule? Don't panic, and do immediately inform your key stake-holders; they trust you and know you to be reliable (the one with the plan). Get them involved in brainstorming alternatives, such as getting extra help, relieving you of other duties, scaling back the scope of the project, and reprioritizing the task to determine which elements are essential and which can wait. De-cluttering your mind and effective time planning will give you room to concentrate on results.

Recognizing Procrastination

Recognizing procrastination is the first step to overcoming one of the greatest barriers to getting things done. How often do you find yourself thinking about a project or task that you need to begin but keep delaying? How much time is spent worrying and feeling guilty over your inability to move the project forward? Do you focus on the small things, such as cleaning your desk drawer or processing your e-mail instead of working on important tasks? If the answer is "a lot" or "yes," then you are a procrastinator and you are not alone. A procrastinator can put off anything, at anytime, and anywhere. It is a special skill that wastes lots of energy and time. It takes procrastinators years of practice to develop and perfect the various subtle tactics that delay and distract them from tackling important tasks. These tactics are often reinforced by carefully cultivated misperceptions (or lies) that disguise the underlying fears—fear of failure, fear of success, fear of saying "no," or fear of rejection—that drive procrastination.

Procrastination Lie No. 1: "It's got to be *PERFECT* or I shouldn't do it at all!"

People who are perfectionists often become absorbed in the details of project control. As a result, they ignore moving it along until the last minute. In this way, they avoid facing their fear of imperfection if the task isn't done. Perfectionism is the ultimate delay tactic because perfection does not exist. The belief that there is always an opportunity to improve can sabotage any project.

Dealing with perfectionism—in yourself or in others—is a delicate operation. My first boss was not a perfectionist—he was the exact opposite. He had a 20-inch by 30-inch Nike poster on the wall of his office that read, "Just Do It!" and was less concerned with the detail and more focused on getting things done. Not only was he an intimidating man with a short fuse, but he also disdained perfectionists. His tactic for dealing with them was to turn their fear of imperfection to a fear of not meeting his deadline. This tactic worked some of the time, but more often, the perfectionist would just quit. I disagreed with his tactics, but recognized that the desire to have everything perfect can be immobilizing. Basically, it is far better (and more realistic) to be effective than it is to be perfect. As a manager, you should try to communicate this to your staff, and understand it for yourself. You can be detailed oriented *and* find it "perfectly" acceptable to aim for optimum solutions, not perfect ones. Perfectionists should lower their standards and praise themselves when the work gets done.

Procrastination Lie No. 2: "I work best under pressure."

Every day someone says he works best "under pressure." It may be a colleague who is considered to be excellent at crisis management, but in reality, no one works best under pressure. Any good management book will tell you that it is better to be proactive than reactive. Although crisis management is certainly a valued skilled in any workplace, no one should choose to use this as their standard operating mode. Public health professionals know this when it comes to hurricane preparedness but can forget it when it comes to their own day-to-day professional lives. When you only react to problems as they occur, you lose your freedom to choose. A good manager wants choice to ensure that resources and time are used optimally. If crisis management is using up too much of your time, take control and prevent "fires" by thinking through projects, especially the ones you assign to others. Proactively work out a plan so that you have time to work on the important things.

Procrastination Lie No. 3: "It is a lot faster and easier if I just do it myself."

The inability to delegate can create huge bottlenecks in getting things done and is the most severe symptom of perfectionism. What is the real worry here, that the task will not get done, or that it will not get done exactly as you want it? As long as you set clear expectations and realistic goals, delegation provides an opportunity to develop employees by expanding their authority and responsibility. It's also an opportunity to strengthen your support base, but you must be willing to allow for mistakes. Plan for mistakes and mitigate their impact by requiring regular progress reports and checkpoint meetings.

Mastering delegation is the primary goal of anyone who aspires to a management position. Effective delegation can further your own goals at the same time that it releases your time for more important work. That said, you need to make sure that you are delegating and neither micromanaging nor "dumping." If you can delegate in a supportive but not obtrusive manner, you will be perceived by your members as a fair and worthy leader. If you delegate but then micromanage, the benefits to you and your colleagues are lost. And finally, if you "dump" your work on them without supporting them with clear, realistic expectations, you will be resented and avoided.

Time Wasters

Wasting time is a sure and common sign of procrastination. As creatures of habit, we waste time in the same way every day. Take the time to identify your top time wasters and eliminate them. Here is a list of common time wasters in the workplace today, in no particular order:

- Ineffective delegation
- Inability to say "No"
- Telephone/e-mail interruptions
- Personal use of Internet
- Inadequate planning
- Poor communication
- Drop-in visitors
- Personal disorganization
- Lack of self-discipline

Which are the biggest time wasters for you? Which do you experience the most difficulty in managing? Why? Become aware of your favorite procrastination tactics. These are all interruptions that prevent you from tackling a project. Also, every time your concentration is broken, you must reorient yourself, which is itself a big waste of time.

You can prevent interruptions when you realize their causes and how much time they consume. Set up your environment with as few distractions as possible. Try delegating time to those things that, if you did not control them, would eat up all your time. For example, to avoid disorganization, clean your desk at the same time every day, and allocate only five minutes to this task. Set your e-mail account so that it does not alert you with every new e-mail, and then set certain times to check and respond to e-mail. When someone asks you for a favor, always say, "I must think about whether I have time," rather than immediately saying yes.

People choose to procrastinate for many different reasons, and procrastination takes many forms. Now that you know how procrastination works and what causes it, you can overcome it. Here are the simple steps:

1. Realize that you are delaying something unnecessarily.
2. Try to understand why you are procrastinating. List the reasons.
3. Dispute the excuses and overcome them.
4. Create an action plan.
5. Begin the task.

When you deal with the underlying reasons for procrastination and sharpen your time management skills, you gain the benefits of more time, reduced stress, and greater efficiency.

Chapter 10

Emotional Intelligence in the Workplace

Claudia S. Plaisted Fernandez

Traditional public health training does a good job at preparing professionals with the requisite "hard" technical skills they need to protect the public's health. But most traditional training programs do not excel at teaching that other critical ingredient, the *soft skills*.

Hard skills are the easy ones, the ones you had classes in way back in school. They are the budget and strategic issues, the scientific application to surveillance, assessment, and care—those issues of fact finding and data recall that represent the technical sides of the field. People with good technical skills often get ahead and progress well through the early stages of their careers. However, people with poor soft skills often derail later in their careers. Soft skills relate to those sticky areas that cause organizational problems—the interpersonal issues.

What Is Emotional Intelligence?

Reuven Bar-On labels these skills collectively as "emotional intelligence" and describes them as an array of noncognitive (emotional and social) capabilities, competencies, and skills that influence one's ability to succeed in coping with environmental demands and pressures.[1,2] Emotional intelligence is more than having a thick skin or a sense of

Chapter Source: © 2007 Wolters Kluwer Health | Lippincott Williams & Wilkins. Originally published in J Public Health Management Practice. 2007; 13(1): 80–82.

empathy for others. It is a genuine ability to feel emotions in response to others, understand what you are feeling, understand how others are feeling, and to move forward constructively with the interests of the larger group at heart. It has to do with building bridges and alliances—and mending those bridges and alliances if they get damaged. The ability to empathize, be resilient in the face of difficulty, and manage one's impulses and stress all fall into the realm of emotional intelligence. In other words, emotional intelligence enables us to make our way in a complex world.

The emotional intelligence quotient, or EQ, has emerged as a tool to describe how one uses their soft skills. It is at the core of much of the leadership literature these days and is a great focus of research for business and industry leaders as well as human resource departments.

Reflect on the five most challenging work situations you have faced. How many represent budget woes or strategic planning issues? How many revolve around the results of faulty communication, organizational culture problems, the inability of individuals to understand one another, or their inability to grasp the effects of their own actions or inaction? While we all have faced budget headaches, it is those latter situations that are the stuff of most organizational migraines.

As a public health manager, you can reap benefits from understanding, exercising, and developing your emotional intelligence. First, EQ is not intelligence quotient, or IQ. Intelligence quotient is concerned with one's capacity to understand information, to learn new information, to recall data, and to think rationally. EQ is also not aptitude, achievement, vocational interest, or personality. Are you reading this laundry list and thinking, "Well, that basically sums up everything that is important in the world?" Think again.

In *The EQ Edge*,[3] psychologist Steven Stein and psychiatrist Howard Book discuss how success at work is related to both IQ and EQ. They note that IQ has been shown to predict an average of 6% of success in a given job, while EQ has been shown to be directly responsible for between 27% and 45% of job success (depending on the field under study). The authors note that having a high IQ and an underdeveloped EQ can hold an otherwise smart professional back, arguing that a high IQ cannot impress people who have been driven away by an abrasive personality or an inability to handle stress.

Our understanding of the neurological basis for some of these phenomena was aided by a case study based on a railway construction accident in 1848 in Cavendish, Vermont.[4] On September 13th of that year, a young foreman named Phineas Gage, capable and efficient, a shrewd and smart businessman, met with tragedy: an accidental explosion from a charge that he had set blew his tamping iron right through his head. The 13.5-pound iron rod took with it much of the left front side of his brain. Reports show that, surprisingly, Gage did not lose consciousness and that, after some months of recuperation, he returned to work. Unfortunately, his personality had changed so much that his previous employers would not rehire him. As Gage expert Malcolm Macmillan reports, poor Phineas Gage was now described as "fitful, irreverent, and grossly profane, showing little deference for his fellows. He was also impatient and obstinate, yet capricious and vacillating, unable to settle on any of the plans he devised for future action. His friends said he was 'No longer Gage.'"

Today, the concept that a part of the brain actually governs—in a predictable way—how emotions are processed and shared with the outside world led psychologists, such as Daniel Goleman,[5] to develop the theory and research on emotional intelligence. And while IQ and personality are static, relatively unchanging components of who we are, our emotional intelligence turns out to be something we can nurture and develop.

Emotional intelligence development is one of the most common reasons people seek executive coaching: strong EQ skills can give one a competitive advantage in the workplace and make work life far more pleasant. As Peter Drucker stresses in *Management Challenges for the 21st Century*, self-awareness and the capacity to build mutually satisfying relationships provide the backbone of strong management.[6]

Know Yourself

EQ experts group the major skills of emotional intelligence into the arenas of *personal* competence—self-awareness and self-management—and *social* competence—social awareness and relationship management. The latter builds on the former. One important point about knowing yourself: it is not about being perfect or having complete control over your emotions; rather it is about understanding your feelings and how they guide your behavior—for better or for worse. The biggest obstacle most people face in developing their EQ is the distinct discomfort that comes from facing up to one's own shortcomings, or "self-awareness." Seeing yourself accurately can sting the sensitivities somewhat, but it is a necessary ingredient to EQ growth.[7,8]

Managers with good emotional intelligence make getting the best out of their direct reports look easy. They are good at motivating others, solving conflict, helping others reduce their stress, and communicating both "up" and "down" on the organizational ladder. As you can see, these are some of the most important skills you can have.

How to Develop Emotional Intelligence

By now you are probably wondering what your EQ is and how you can nurture it. The most accepted tool measuring EQ is called the Bar-On Emotional Quotient Inventory, or EQi.[1] This instrument breaks EQ down into five major areas and 15 minor ones, or subscales. The five overarching areas include intrapersonal (dealing with yourself), interpersonal (dealing with others), stress management, adaptability, and general mood. The instrument is used in targeted selection programs to match EQ with job fit for several industries, including the U.S. military, the FBI, insurance firms, and customer service divisions of corporations. It is used in many leadership and management development programs, such as the Southeast Public Health Leadership Institute, the Food Systems Leadership Institute, as well as executive coaching programs.

Short of enrolling in a leadership institute or an executive coaching session, a good way to understand and develop your own EQ is to reflect on what seems to make the difference for others who are successful and focus on those issues for yourself. In a study of 16,222 individuals, five EQi subscale categories emerged as significantly related to overall work success. These include self-actualization, optimism, stress tolerance, happiness, and assertiveness. Let us look at these in more detail.

Self-actualization is the ability to realize one's potential capacities and to lead a rich and meaningful life. The theory goes that people who feel a sense of fulfillment work harder, are more pleasant to be around, and have an edge on productivity and teamwork.

Optimism and stress tolerance have to do with how you handle adversity and challenges. How you "muddle through" when adversity cannot be avoided is what is important. Optimism is defined as the ability to look at the brighter side of life and to maintain a positive attitude even in the face of adversity. People who can still see the light at the end of the tunnel or the silver lining are not easily defeated and demoralized by the bumps and bruises along the way.

Similarly, stress tolerance is the ability to withstand adverse events and stressful situations without falling apart, the use of coping strategies to weather difficult situations and avoid being overwhelmed by adversity. Certainly, getting overwhelmed and falling apart has a negative relationship with productivity at work.

Happiness is a somewhat surprising EQ strength for success at work. Who knew that the ability to feel satisfied with one's life, to enjoy oneself and others, and to have fun would improve work performance? The theory is that happy people show enthusiasm at both play and work and that this attitude infuses their relationships. Happy people can easily attract and build relationships with others, according to the research of Stein and Book,[3] while people who are sad have little enthusiasm or energy to share with their colleagues, and both their work and their relationships show it.

Assertiveness, the final of the top five, is more complex. It involves three major components of standing up for yourself, with the common characteristics that this is done in a nondestructive manner and maintained even if the stance taken is not popular. Assertiveness is (1) the ability to express one's feelings, (2) to express thoughts and beliefs openly (even if it is emotionally difficult to do so and even if there is personal risk involved), and (3) to stand up for one's personal rights by not allowing others to bother or take advantage of you. It is the opposite of shyness, and it is the opposite of abusiveness or aggressiveness. People who are assertive can arrive at a constructive compromise, creating the much-sought-after win-win solution. They can walk the fine line, defending their deeply held beliefs, disagreeing with others, and not resorting to emotional sabotage or subterfuge. They respect the other person's point of view and are sensitive to their needs. Sounds like a tough recipe? Well, the most successful people at work have figured that one out.

So if you want to get ahead, to inspire your direct reports to make the most of their talents, and to maximize your own productivity, then perhaps taking another course on budgets or epidemiological evidence is not what you really need. Perhaps it is time to take stock of your happiness, your stress level, your ability to constructively give voice to your views, to be fulfilled, and to have fun. Perhaps it is time to use the EQ framework to take more than a passing glance at that silver lining and give more weight to the bright side of attitude. We encourage you to learn more about EQ. After all, it is what your successful peers are doing. They—and their colleagues—are better off for it.

References

1. Bar-On R. *Bar-On Emotional Quotient Inventory (EQ-i) Manual.* Toronto: Multi-Health Systems; 1997.

2. Bar-On R. The Bar-On Model of emotional-social intelligence (ESI). In: Fernandez-Berrocal P, Extremera N, eds. *Special Issue on Emotional Intelligence. Psicothema.* 17;2005. Available at: www.eiconsortium.org. Accessed December 17, 2008.

3. Stein SJ, Book HE. *The EQ Edge: Emotional Intelligence and your Success.* Mississuaga, Ontario, Canada: John Wiley & Sons; 2006.

4. Macmillan M. The Phineas Gage information page. Australia, Victoria: School of Psychology, Deakin University. Available at: www.deakin.edu.au/hmnbs/psychology/gagepage/index.php. Accessed December 17, 2008.

5. Goleman D. *Emotional Intelligence: Why It Can Matter More Than IQ.* New York, NY: Bantam Dell; 2005.

6. Drucker PF. *Management Challenges for the 21st Century.* 1st ed. New York: HarperCollins Publishers; 1999.

7. Mayer JD, Salovey P, Caruso D. *Mayer-Salovey-Caruso Emotional Intelligenc eTests (MSCEIT) User's Manual.* Toronto: Multi-Health Systems; 2002.

8. Lynn AB. *The Emotional Intelligence Activity Book: 50 Activities for Promoting EQ at Work.* HRD Press; 2002.

9. Hayden T. Renaissance Resources, Brunswick County, NC. *The Star-News.* Available at: www.starnewsonline.com. Accessed December 17, 2008.

Chapter 11

Creating Thought Diversity: The Antidote to Groupthink

Claudia S. Plaisted Fernandez

W e hear a lot about the importance of diversity in the workplace these days. You may think that having a diverse workforce is just a way to "look like" the population you serve. You may promote diversity because you have to or because it's politically correct. But the most important reason to promote diversity is because a diverse group of people brings diverse ways of thinking about things. And you can build "thought diversity" no matter who you have at the table.

Thought diversity allows for differing perspectives on ideas and unique insights into problems. It creates opportunities for innovation, entrepreneurship, and partnerships in unexpected places. It allows you to take a "reality check" before plunging into new activities. Most important, it helps you avoid *groupthink*.

Thought Diversity over Groupthink

Groupthink occurs when one or two people or personality styles dominate a group's culture so completely that there is no room for those with other styles, perspectives, needs, or beliefs to get their ideas on the table. This can take the form of people hiring only those who think

Chapter Source: © 2007 Wolters Kluwer Health | Lippincott Williams & Wilkins. Originally published in *J Public Health Management Practice.* 2007; 13(6): 670–671.

as they do or dominant thinkers badgering others into accepting their ideas, critically downplaying the value of others' ideas, or simply failing to listen.

In groupthink, conformity reigns supreme. The group will make great sacrifices to simply get along and maintain the peace and harmony within. Often the group overestimates its own power and morality: what they are doing is *right*, and their track record of success is so strong that they do not consider the possibility of failure.[1,2]

Public health and public health research are not immune to the problems of groupthink. Whenever we fail to examine a problem from all angles and rigorously question our actions, we invite narrowly thought-out options to rule the day. Whenever we say, "This is the way we've always done it," and fail to encourage open discussion and alternative ideas, we put our organizations at risk of groupthink. So how does a manager create a thought-diverse organizational culture? Here is a seven-step plan to improving thought diversity.

Seven Steps to Create Thought Diversity and Avoid Groupthink

1. Encourage open discussion.
2. Explore all problems from the four-point *sequence*.
3. Assign roles for asking difficult questions (have a devil's advocate).
4. Reward truth speakers.
5. Tool your staff for the art of the difficult conversation.
6. Invite new perspectives to the discussion.
7. Build in time to reflect and revisit tough decisions.

In Step 1, encourage open discussion. To do this, do not control the discussion or state your outcome expectations at the outset. Explain that the goal of the process is to understand the ideas completely, which requires their thorough examination. To facilitate this examination, I recommend that groups engage in Step 2: examine issues from a four-point sequence.

Point A: Ask questions about the known data, including what facts describe the situation? What can we learn from the past? And what relevant experience do others have that we could learn from?

Point B: The group explores any themes that emerge from the data. Understanding these themes can help your team understand the big picture and also point out possibilities or options for other strategies.

Point C: List the criteria for making a good decision, and chart the pros and cons of each option. Acknowledging the most logical solution will be helpful, but don't let that dominate this process.

Point D: Brainstorm who else the group must collaborate with or learn from to solve the problem. Analyze how the proposed solutions will affect the stakeholders, both those within the organization and others. Which solution will promote maximum acceptance by stakeholders, including the general public? Following Points A through D will help your team go far in avoiding groupthink.

In Step 3, encourage diversity of thought. Assign someone to play the devil's advocate, the person who will ask "reality check" questions. It is uncomfortable to look at worst-case scenarios, but it can be devastating to turn a blind eye to them. Questions might include: What if we fail to achieve this goal? What if the current conditions change—and change our resource base? Are we measuring success by the right metrics? What are the undesirable effects this endeavor will create? This devil's advocate function requires a great deal of bravery on the part of the individual who might face censure from other group members. With Step 4, reward those truth speakers and make sure that they have the skills to play the whistleblower tactfully and tastefully.

Step 5 calls on managers and leaders to equip their whole team with the tools to conduct difficult conversations. Often people can become passionate about their ideas. When they do, they can become personally identified with them, and then criticism of the idea feels personal. You, as manager, must set the stage that this process is not about people but about ideas. The discussions are to strengthen the ideas from within before they become programs or policies that are put into play publicly or organization-wide.

In Step 6, if you find that you continue to have the same old discussions, then as leadership and organizational development expert Meg Wheatley states,[3] change the people at the table. To create a new culture for discussion you might need to change those sharing ideas. Explore having nonvoting members attend management meetings to represent other views or invite nontraditional community stakeholders to the discussion.

In Step 7, the process is to avoid rushing to judgment. Premature closure will end up costing the organization more time and other resources than will giving adequate time for reflection. Difficult choices warrant time for reflection and revisiting the decision-making process. Challenge the decisions made and the processes followed, and ensure that all ideas are considered. In the long run, it is better to answer the difficult questions about your decision-making process than it is to explain the inadequacies in it.

Summary

When organizations embrace diversity of thought, it is easier for diversity in all its other forms to follow. Creating an organization culture that welcomes discussion, is respectful of disagreement, and encourages mutual exploration of ideas contributes to creating a learning organization. Furthermore, it positions the organization to capitalize on innovation and partnerships that can keep it where it needs to be: on the cutting edge of discovery and delivery of services.

References

1. Griffin E. *Groupthink.* New York: McGraw-Hill; 1997.
2. Rounds J. Groupthink. Available at: http://www.colostate.edu/Depts/Speech/rccs/theory16.htm. Published 2000. Accessed May 25, 2007.
3. Wheatley M. How can you maintain leadership direction and focus in these turbulent times? Presented at: Public Health Leadership Institute; May 2007; Chapel Hill, NC.

Section **II**

Managing
Partnerships

Chapter 12

Partnering Essentials

Janet E. Porter and Edward L. Baker, Jr.

"Strong partnerships among government, communities, philanthropies, and the corporate community to facilitate actions to improve the health of employees and their communities are critical for the public health system to improve its goals."[1] Despite this proclamation from the Institute of Medicine and the efforts of Turning Point and the National Study of Partnership Functioning,[2] public health officials generally do not demonstrate effective partnership skills. Increasingly, the ability to effectively leverage community resources to tackle intransigent community issues—gang crime, domestic violence, drug abuse, teenage pregnancy—is seen as the differentiating leadership competency. For partnerships to last and have impact, the relationship has to be seen as far more than just a sharing of resources and risk. The relationship has to be an exchange of perspectives about the nature of the challenge and possible solutions such that the resultant whole is really greater than the parts.

We will review "Partnering 101: What, Why, When, Who, How," and test your perspective and skills. We will return to this subject in the next few chapters because this essential competency is too fundamental to cover just once.

Chapter Source: © 2005 Wolters Kluwer Health | Lippincott Williams & Wilkins. Originally published in *J Public Health Management Practice.* 2005; 11(2): 174–177.

The First Successful Ingredient of a Partnership: Humility

First, whether it is an individual or a business, an organization or a company, a church or a public health agency, the decision to partner requires humility. You have to recognize your own limitations and admit that working with another will more likely result in success than going it alone. Like the Lone Ranger, understanding that he was better able to capture the bad guys in the wild, wild West with Tonto at his side, you have to appreciate that you need help to accomplish your objectives. Some professions thrive on partnerships; Rogers and Hammerstein are only one of numerous successful duos of composers and lyricists who made beautiful music together, and Bob Hope and Bing Crosby represent a long line of comedic pairs who have brought us laughter.

Humility also requires that you appreciate the perspective you bring to the project, which is based on your professional education, your age, your past experience, your gender, and your ethnic background. The true value of partnerships—which is that each organization and individual will bring their own perspective to the project—can only be realized if individuals are open to approaching a problem. Of course, humility means not only knowing your limitations but also knowing your strengths—as they say in marketing, your distinctive competency. What is it that you bring to the table, that you contribute that would make someone want to partner with you on a new initiative? Think about it from the partner's perspective. Would they agree that you have demonstrated expertise at working effectively with community groups, spreading a public health message, or delivering services to the community? If you cannot come up with concrete examples that illustrate your distinctive competencies, then you may not be able to sell potential partners on working with you.

Honest reflection requires humility because along with your strengths, you may bring baggage to a partnership. You may have a previous history of poor collaboration or failed ventures. Of course, if you have learned valuable lessons from failed initiatives, that means you are smarter entering this new partnership and you can turn that experience into a strength, not a weakness.

One of the major lessons from Peter Senge's work on learning organizations is that organizations committed to self-improvement stop and evaluate how they are doing all the time. For learning to occur, regular reflection is a must. In partnerships, reflection often takes place as debriefings after project milestones. For those debriefings to be truly insightful, partners must be prepared to honestly admit their shortcomings and failures, and those admissions can only come from partners with humility. The North Carolina Institute for Public Health had a partnership with the Research Triangle Institute and other schools on campus to conduct a joint feasibility study about establishing a national patient safety improvement corps. The intense, 9-month project was challenging. A director left midway through the project, and the partners had conflicting views about the intention and format of the project. Nevertheless, the partners deemed the project a huge success because of the cathartic two-hour debriefing, at which partners shared their personal epiphanies. People feel good about partnership experiences when they have learned something and there is a sense of closure and accomplishment. People bond through adversity. Structured reflection throughout the project, but especially at the conclusion, provides an opportunity for emotional bonding, healing, and learning.

Sharing a Unifying, Compelling Goal

Public health partnerships form around a community need that may have been invisible to many of the partners for some time. Oftentimes, a sentinel event occurs—a crisis in funding, the unnecessary death of a teenage girl from an illegal abortion, rising community unrest leading to gang activity, or a dire report rating the community as one of the worst in the state in suicide, tuberculosis, HIV—which drives partners to action. In the case of the Partnership for Migrant and Seasonal Farm Worker Health in Idaho, it was a trip to Mexico by the Boise Sunrise Rotary Club and the executive director of the Family Advocacy Program that made them question whether their local migrant workers had as high an incidence of preventable eye disorders as they had seen in Mexico.[3]

The primary responsibility of the convening partner is to illustrate the magnitude of the problem—to paint such a compelling picture that everyone invited joins the initiative. The magnitude of the program can be conveyed through data, but humanizing this issue through stories is essential to engage people in the passion of the project.

After seeing the problem in the community, rather than being overwhelmed by the need, the partners' challenge is to be stimulated into action. What creates that positive energy? Leaders who tell stories of hope create a sense of possibility. They provide examples of how other communities have tackled similar problems. One of the best ways to sell a new initiative to partners, funders, and community leaders is to share a success story or program that you can use as a model. Franchises are such a successful business model for expanding from one location to numerous locations because all the key stakeholders can use the first location as a model. Starbucks, which essentially sells colored, flavored water, is just the latest example of a wildly successful food franchise that started with one profitable location.

Partners come to an initial meeting with their own agenda and perspective on what should be accomplished. Skilled facilitation enables a group to coalesce around a clear and compelling common goal. Once that is accomplished, a partnership is formed when the members of the group dedicate themselves and resources to meaningful activities and measurable outcomes grounded in a compelling mission. The 24 partners in the Galveston (Texas) Community Health Access Program attribute the success of the initiative, which won the 2004 National Campus-Community Partnerships for Health Award, to "bringing the right people and organizations to the table to organize *around a single goal* . . . to bridge gaps in access to health care in Galveston County."[4]

Sharing Risk

The third essential element of a successful partnership is *shared risk*. As they say in sports, everyone has to have "skin in the game." This does not mean that all the partners have the same investment or the same risk exposure, but it does mean that everyone commits resources—staff support, access to databases, connections to key community stakeholders—to make sure the venture is successful. Public health partners tend to discount their ability to contribute to a partnership because of limited financial resources when in fact their intangible resources—connections with key community leaders and organizations or access to data illustrating community need—can be equally valuable in the success of a new community initiative. When we discuss partner selection in Chapter 14, we'll talk about selecting partners on the basis of their ability and willingness to contribute and share risk.

For some partners, sharing risk makes it even more difficult to let go of the daily management of the shared project. Although a dozen or more organizations may come together to sponsor a public health community initiative, typically one organization will actually take the lead, providing the space, employing the managerial staff, and providing day-to-day direction. The other partners need to view themselves in a governing role that provides strategic direction, establishes policy, and ensures financial viability, but they also need to feel comfortable delegating the managerial details to the management and lead sponsor. Letting go requires trust. In our leadership courses at the University of North Carolina (UNC), we regularly schedule participants to do the ropes course. On the high ropes, when public health leaders are dangling 20 feet off the ground, depending on teammates to guide them to other side, they learn that they have to let go of being in control and to allow others to guide them to success. For partners to let go of how the project will be managed, they have to trust that the lead partners have placed the interests of the initiative first and have the skills to execute the project.

Building Trust

The fourth essential element of successful partnerships is trust. First, trust is a function of both the person trusting (the trustee) and the person being trusted (the "trustor"). The innate perceptions, skills, history, and experience of the trustee is just as important as the ability of the trustor to deliver as promised. If partners come to the potential project with memories of bad experience from previous partnerships, their innate lack of trust and unwillingness can be just as damaging to the partnership as the actual failure to deliver. We all know what a fragile thing trust is. Once lost, "All the Kings' horses and all the Kings' men, couldn't put Humpty Dumpty together again." Nothing better cements trust than honest communication, and nothing destroys trust more quickly than lying. In a recent discussion of a failed merger of two Catholic hospitals, one sister, who was CEO of one of the organizations, said, "The issue was dead the minute we learned they had $40 million in debt they had deliberately hidden from us. We talked for several months, but it was just wasted breath."

Trust is also based on believing that individuals can and will deliver on commitments. More than honesty is required for successful execution; knowing key stakeholders in their respective organizations, being able to assess the political landscape, and having the authority to allocate resources are also important elements of trust. When partners trust, they believe that each partner is going to follow through, to do what they say they are going to do. And this is even more difficult because, throughout the life of a project, environmental forces constantly change the options, the direction, the pace of the project.

Like a Seesaw

Trust is built by honesty and the ability to execute and also by partners demonstrating a heartfelt interest in making sure all the partners are heard and considered in planning a venture. Masterful leadership is necessary to ensure that partners' expectations are realistic and that the rewards are balanced. One of the elements that a leader is striving for in a partnership is *reciprocity*. If you recognize the absolute importance of each partner to the venture's success, the time will come when you will have to put your organization's interests second to the interests of the partnership or another partner's needs. Just like in friendship, as Stephen Covey says, you invest in others by making deposits in their emotional bank accounts so that when you want to make a withdrawal, there is a balance.

The UNC Kenan Institute and the School of Public Health established a partnership six years ago to offer the Management Academy for Public Health.[3] This was the first sizable partnership between these two schools in the history of the university. The original $2.8 million grant was awarded to the School of Public Health, and thus the School got "credit"—in the way that universities count awards for the grant. Now, these same partners are offering the Emerging Leaders in Public Health Program[5] funded by the W. K. Kellogg Foundation, and the award has been granted to the Kenan Institute so they can get "credit" at UNC for this grant award. This is reciprocity in action.

Leadership

Finally, the essential element of a successful partnership is *leadership*. As the National Study of Partnership Functioning discovered from studying 66 partnerships, "leadership effectiveness was the dimension . . . most closely related to partnership synergy. This finding is consistent with other research that has documented the importance of leadership across all phases of partnership development."[2] As Jim Collins articulates in *Good to Great*,[6] developing a new program or service is like getting people on a bus to go on a trip. The leader's goal is to motivate followers to get on the bus by painting a picture of a compelling vision—an attractive destination, a reason for going on the trip, a reason for departing from their current location. Throughout the journey, when there are many twists and turns, flat tires, bad roadside food, and unspeakable bathroom breaks, the leader's job is to keep the group focused on the ultimate destination. It requires trust and flexibility to let go of the details of how long the journey will take or which route will be followed and to remain clear about the group's mission to focus on the destination.

Leaders not only motivate and engage partners, they also develop a communication strategy. Knowing how much and what the partners want to know, how involved they want to be in decision making, and how often they want updates is an essential leadership skill. Trust and communication are reciprocal; with little trust, there needs to be more communication; with lots of trust, communication can be sparse. When we talk about partnership management in subsequent chapters, we'll discuss tips for effective partnership communication.

In the following chapters, we'll discuss picking partners and the importance of complementarity to develop the ideal partnership. In the meantime, take a moment to ask yourself these questions before you establish a partnership to address a pressing community need:

- Are you realistic and humble about your need for others to help with this initiative?
- Can you paint a compelling picture for the partners of this need?
- Are you willing to share risk?
- Are you trustworthy in partnerships?
- Are you flexible about the ways this partnership is formed, executes strategies, and measures results?
- Do you have the leadership skills necessary to convene a community group around a need? If not, then who can you engage to lead this dream to becoming a reality?

References

1. Institute of Medicine. *The Future of the Public's Health in the 21st Century.* Washington, D.C.: National Academies Press; 2003:300.
2. Weiss E, Anderson R, Lasker R. Making the most of collaboration: exploring the relationship between partnership synergy and partnership functioning. *Health Educ Behav.* 2002;29(6):683–698.
3. Boise State University Nursing. Spring 2002 Idaho migrant and seasonal farm worker health fair. Available at: http://nursing.boisestate.edu/department/migrant%5Fworkers.htm. Accessed November 2, 2004.
4. University of Texas Medical branch, Office of Community Outreach. Galveston County Health Access Program. Available at: http://www.galvestonchap.org. Accessed November 2, 2004.

5. North Carolina Institute for Public Health, School of Public Health, University of North Carolina at Chapel Hill and Kenan-Flagler Business School, University of North Carolina at Chapel Hill. Managing in turbulent times: Kellogg Fellowship for emerging leaders in public health. Available at: http://publichealthleaders.org. Accessed November 2, 2004.

6. Collins J. *Good to Great: Why Some Companies Make the Leap...and Others Don't.* New York: HarperCollins; 2001.

Chapter 13

Humility and Technology to Foster Partnerships

Janet E. Porter and Stephen N. Orton

In the previous chapter, six elements essential for a successful partnership were analyzed. Five of the six elements—setting goals, sharing risk and rewards, building trust and leadership—probably sound familiar. But we hope that thinking about the importance of the virtue enumerated by Benjamin Franklin in his autobiography—humility—stimulated reflection on your own successes and failures with leveraging others to accomplish public health goals in your community. While lack of humility is a barrier to partnerships, there is no question that technological breakthroughs have served to facilitate communication among partners. In this chapter, we will explore further lack of humility as a barrier to successful partnerships and the use of technology to communicate as a facilitator of partnerships.

A Culture of Individualism—Not Humility

Being humble means knowing your own limitations as a manager and the limitations of your organization. Being humble means knowing that you cannot achieve your goals alone. And being humble means revealing those limitations to others, a critical step toward finding compensatory strengths in other people and in other organizations.

Chapter Source: © 2005 Lippincott Williams & Wilkins, Inc. Originally published in *J Public Health Management Practice.* 2005; 11(3): 252–255.

Americans like to think of themselves as good teammates: our culture puts high value on teamwork. We love watching team sports like football. We pride ourselves on our tolerance and our ability to overlook differences, as the "melting pot" image suggests. We like to imagine ourselves pulling together in a crisis and confronting problems rationally and effectively as a group. But that is only part of our cultural foundation regarding teamwork.

Our culture also resists teamwork. Strong individuals like Lance Armstrong who pursue "solo" sports are celebrated, and their accomplishments are described as though they triumphed alone—even though Lance had a great team of cyclists to help him win his Tour de France (and a great team of healthcare workers to help him beat cancer). Even in sports that clearly depend on team effort, superstars are selected for special praise, such as quarterbacks, who typically spend half the game sitting on the bench, or wide receivers, who might touch only the ball six or eight times a game. We seek out and praise pioneers, striking out into the wilderness alone.

Enormous credit is given to individuals who lead huge organizations, such as Steve Jobs at Apple, whose personal success and cultural status clearly depend on the exertions of thousands of other people: Apple employees and partners who design intuitive buttons that feel good, create new plastics, develop hardware and software, figure out manufacturing logistics, make sales, create marketing buzz, and so on. It is easy to forget that companies such as Apple (or football teams and public health agencies) are composed of many people moving in the same direction.

Apple's success is a victory of teamwork. Imagine the management task of deploying the army of organizations necessary to develop the constituent parts of a functioning piece of modern technology, say, the iPod: the effort not only of engineers who know about batteries, audio, disk drives, and LCD panels but also designers who know about materials and aesthetics and human interface issues, managers who know about human resources and international trade laws and logistics, and software developers who know about interfaces between multiple different operating systems. Having conceived of the machine—an incredibly complex task—it had to be adapted to customers. Marketers had to understand the market for portable music players— who would buy which configuration at what price—and convince people to use a new, very different, and expensive version. Finally, someone had to negotiate with musicians. The iTunes Web site was a critical piece of the puzzle in building the success of the iPod because it brings iPod users directly into contact with music creators.

In other words, the success of the iPod is due to some lucky timing but also due to the efforts of a huge team: many players, from many different disciplines (engineers to managers to artists) and from many different companies and suppliers, with great ideas and great skills. The leadership developing the iPod had to know what they could do well and where they needed help. They did not assume that they alone could make it happen. They were humble. In some ways, Apple serves as merely the "convener" for this group of innovators. Public health managers often perform this role in the community health arena.

Jim Collins's research in *Good to Great: Why Some Companies Make the Leap and Others Don't* further supports the importance of humility for organization success. Collins has conducted exhaustive research of 1435 companies to determine which have had the best sustained financial performance over decades. Then his research team analyzed which factors these seemingly disparate but great companies—Walgreens, Kimberly Clark, Kroger, Abbott, Circuit City—have in common. "Level 5 leadership" is the first factor he describes as common among these great companies. Essentially, these companies were all led by "level 5 leaders," who "built enduring greatness through a paradoxical blend of personal humility and professional will."[1]

That same combination of leadership characteristics—humility plus dogged persistence—distinguishes community initiatives that succeed from those that fail. But just as humility is essential for leadership, communication is essential for trust.

Technology Facilitates the Other Key Element—Communication

We live in a time of great technological change. In the past 15 years, the personal computer revolution that spurred big gains in worker productivity has allowed an even greater revolution in communication to take place. In 1992, only 2% of the U.S. population used e-mail; the first Windows-based e-mail program did not hit the market until 1993. Ten years ago, less than 10% of the U.S. population was online. Two years ago, 66% were online, and the percentage is rising. The U.S. Postal Service (despite years of good marketing through their sponsorship of Lance Armstrong's successful Tour de France cycling team) has had usage level off at 100 billion pieces of mail a year; the Internet carries that many e-mail messages in a week. E-mail has clearly changed the way managers communicate.

Thoughtful, risk-taking companies and organizations have learned to take advantage of the possibilities inherent in the Web and e-mail. Amazon.com, for instance, helped show the way to a virtual marketplace by betting that people would want to shop over the Internet. Barack Obama's presidential campaign helped show the possibilities of Internet tools for raising money and organizing political action among huge numbers of people.

Public health organizations have similarly taken advantage of new communication tools: many state health departments now publish restaurant inspection scores on their Web sites, and some, such as Virginia, share full inspection reports (http://www.healthspace .ca/vdh/). On the national level, the Centers for Disease Control and Prevention is sharing evidence-based practice outcomes for various types of public interventions on their Web site (thecommunityguide .org). Think about Amazon.com: they use their Web site not only to talk to people (buy some books!) but to listen as well. Amazon gathers information about you as a customer at each visit and remembers what titles you have bought in the past, how you paid for them, and where you shipped them. Amazon also facilitates customers' communication with one another. Customers provide book lists to other customers; they share opinions on books they liked or did not like; they can even create their own "gift list" pages so that their friends and relatives can buy books for them. The Virginia Department of Health food inspection site similarly serves a dual purpose: it shares government data with everyone in the state, but it also allows inspectors across the state to see how other inspectors are filling out their reports and grading what they find.

And the communication revolution has not just occurred with computers and the Internet. The telecommunications revolution has also enabled communication and, like the Internet, created expectations about the pace at which work gets done and the instant availability of people to get the work done. And the best is yet to come.

Dr. Russell Ackoff of the University of Pennsylvania Wharton School of Business tells his personal transformational story about going to visit a friend at Bell Labs in 1953. It just so happened that the friend's boss—a vice president—had had an epiphany the night before about the lack of technological breakthroughs in telephone communication. Recognizing that all the great innovations—the invention of the dial, simultaneous processing, switching—had been invented more than 50 years earlier, the vice president declared in an early morning meeting that all the PhDs at Bell Labs would quit working immediately on modifications to the current telephone system and instead would "assume the telephone system of the United States was destroyed yesterday." Dividing the group of 60 PhDs into work teams, Russell and his friend were assigned to the team whose task was to design a new instrument—the actual phone in the home or office. Not knowing what to do once they arrived in a lone conference room, it was finally suggested that the team should begin to list features that the phone might have—features that became known as cordless, call waiting, call forwarding, and conferencing. But what is most amazing about Dr. Ackoff's story is that the group of engineers in the course of one day in 1953 identified a list of 67 features for phones—and that 50 years later only two-thirds of those features are readily available in the home or office. So, not only are the means to communicate telephonically easier than ever—we can expect ever more ease because of the further evolution of telecommunications.

All this technology, however, poses a burden. It eliminates any excuses about no or poor communication, and it does not replace the need for some personal interaction to meet individual needs for affiliation. So with technology available to facilitate communication, what are some communication basics in partnerships?

Communication Basics

In the next chapter, we will explore selecting partners, but before analyzing key stakeholders, it is important to think through a communications strategy for your partnership. When responding to a grant opportunity, the tendency is often to leap to the phone to call potential partners to assess their interest and to gain their support. But pausing to think about communication before selecting partners will pay off in terms of both recruiting partners and managing the partnership.

Typically, in establishing a partnership to tackle a community health issue—the rise of sexually transmitted diseases or childhood obesity, for example—attention is paid, rightfully, to crafting a message about community need. Public health agencies have become savvy about optimally using both local and national data to communicate need. Likewise, public health agencies have learned much about message diffusion and using connectors, salespeople, and mavens to spread messages rapidly throughout a community. Communication is really about spreading a message, and public health appreciates the role of informal, random, and personal messages. Even before you determine whom to approach to be a partner, think through your argument for anyone participating in this initiative.

Equally important is brainstorming how you will use technology optimally to share documents, communicate messages to the public, meet regularly, and support joint decision making among the partners. Part of the "pitch" given to potential partners should be the ease with which partners will be able to work together. Something as basic as establishing a contact list for all the partners at the first meeting and then using that to establish a Listserv can make a difference in terms of ensuring that everyone receives the same timely communication, especially early on in the partnerships' evolution, which is critical in building trust. From debriefing more arduous partnerships, we have learned that something as basic as partners' use of different software (Word or WordPerfect) or different versions of the same software can be a nightmare when sharing and editing documents.

The University of California at Berkeley, the Center for Creative Leadership, the Kenan-Flagler Business School, and the School of Public Health created a partnership to design and deliver a national healthcare leadership institute for the National Center for Healthcare Leadership. The partners were recruited partly because their initial time investment would be minimized with Blackboard to share documents and teleconferencing to facilitate shared decision making. At the first meeting of the partnership, the means by which the partners would communicate using Blackboard and the frequency and process for teleconferencing were established, which facilitated rapid execution.

So, before you pick up the phone to call someone to support you in the next initiative, answer the following questions:

1. What is the best argument you can make for the need in your community for this initiative? What data support the need? Can you quantify a realistic outcome?
2. What will the partners gain from participating? Can you build a case for the value of participating in this initiative such that partners will be clamoring to join?
3. What is the fit between the partners' interests, your public health agency interests, and the way you envision this new partnership working?
4. How will the partners work together? How often will they meet? How will they make decisions?
5. What technology can you use to facilitate the partnership? Will there be teleconferences? Will you establish a Listserv? Can you establish a Web site or use a system like Blackboard to share documents?

6. What resources—including technology—do you bring to the partnership and what resources do you need others to provide?
7. What are your lessons learned from previous partnerships? What mistakes were made and how can you make sure they are not repeated?
8. What can you contribute to the initiative? What can you not contribute wherein you will need help from your new partners?

Take a moment not to just think about these questions but to record your answers. They will guide you as you proceed with your new partnership.

Reference

1. Collins J. *Good to Great: Why Some Companies Make the Leap ... and Others Don't.* New York: HarperCollins; 2001:12–13.

Chapter 14

Selecting Partners and Setting the Stage

Janet E. Porter and Edward L. Baker, Jr.

The last few chapters have discussed the elements of public health partnerships. Since collaboration is such a contemporary concept in public health, and teams are such a focus of business success, talking about public health partnerships raises the question, "What is the difference between a partnership, a collaboration, and a team?" We have deliberately selected to focus on public health partnerships because they refer to relationships that are longer term and external. Collaborations tend to be issue specific, shorter term, and less structured. After all, legally, a partnership is a contractual relationship between two or more parties. The reason it makes sense to think in terms of partnerships rather than collaborations is that public health leaders need to think of creating enduring alliances to improve community health. These partnerships need to transcend the public health issue of the moment, the latest funding stream, or personal connection between two leaders and need to be deep-seated organizational commitments to work together on intransigent issues.

Reflecting on whether you have the essential ingredients of a successful partnership—humility, leadership, trust, reciprocity—is a good starting point. But after that reflection, how do you select partners and then sustain those partnerships during the inevitable trials and tribulations? Most of us in public health can draw on personal experience and identify past partnerships that have flourished and left a legacy and others that have not gotten off the ground or been strife with controversy. And sometimes the factors that made the difference between a downward spiral and reaching lofty aims are bewildering.

Selecting Partners

The key to a good partnership—like a good marriage, a good sports team, or competing on *Survivor*—is in whom you pick. This presumes, of course, that you get to pick. Even then, many times, there are dominant organizations in the community that must be partners for an initiative to get off the ground.

What is the best way to get to do the picking? If you are the co-ordinating or initiating partner, you will most likely decide—or play a major role in deciding—who the partners are and what their roles will be. This responsibility requires you to have initiative and connections. Today, one of those connection mechanisms is the Internet. Oftentimes, the secret to being in the know is simply to be on the right Listservs. For example, the National Association of City and County Health Officials and the Turning Point Listservs both provide regular announcements about public health initiatives that might be turned into great community partnerships.

So, once you have decided to launch a new public health initiative, and you are in a position to build the partnership, how do you decide whom to invite? The answer can be summarized in one word: complementarity. Selecting partners who balance your public health agency, who bring resources, expertise, political connections, past experience—especially in the areas where you are lacking—is the key. Part of this goes back to the earlier comments made about humility. You need an honest sense of your own strengths and vulnerabilities to know whom to select as a partner—who will "round you out." Shel Silverstein explores the universal subject of complementarity in his children's book *The Missing Piece*. The main character looks like Ms. Pac-Man, running around looking for a one-sixth piece of the pie to make it whole. Do you need a stronger connection with the emergency services community, the mayor's office, or the neighborhood health centers? Select partners who balance, who complement you, and who give you political strength, resources, or the credibility you need to get the job done.

As with any good party, the question with partners is not just whom to invite but how many. For partnerships to endure, the partners have to have a stake and a personal sense of role or purpose to maintain the commitment. And, you have to intend for them to have a role more than just being letterhead on the stationery. At the North Carolina Institute for Public Health (NCIPH), we recently applied for a $6 million leadership grant for a specific target public health audience we do not know well. Within a few weeks, we pulled together five partners—a school of public health, a state agency, a medical school, a business school, and a historically black university—to customize our leadership development approach to meet the needs of the designated target audience. Every partner contributed enormously to the project concept: one knew the science, another knew about public health at the local level, and another knew about creating sustaining enterprises. We debated at several points whether to add more partners, but finally felt comfortable that the current partners had "all our bases covered." Having more partners would not have added value, and managing the partnership and disbursing the resources gets more complex as the partnership's size grows. It is extremely important to select the right partners and the right number of partners to get the job done efficiently.

The Center for Creative Leadership has studied leadership for 40 years and has become the font of knowledge on the subject. Recently, it has developed and explored the concept of "derailers"— those *personal* characteristics that cause a person to be fired or demoted. Applying this same concept, derailers of partnerships are those characteristics you want to avoid because they likely increase failure. A key derailer in a partnership is just one destructive partner, a partner who detracts from the overall sense of energy to accomplish the mission, who divides the partners into factions, who sees the glass as half empty rather than half full. Another partnership derailer is the lack of an acknowledged credible lead partner. The initiating partner—the organization that calls everyone together initially—may not emerge as the ideal lead partner. This is when egos, self-promotion, and other destructive personal behavior can derail a partnership.

Setting the Stage

Nothing dooms a partnership more than inappropriate expectations. The challenge is to be realistic about outcomes but, at the same time, to have lofty aims. When partners are invited to participate in an initiative, they want to know what role you envision for them, and failure to ask or answer that question will be problematic.

A quick story might illustrate the importance of creating realistic expectations. A phone call came in a few years ago to the NCIPH from the Research Triangle Institute (RTI), asking NCIPH to partner on a proposal. On hearing this news, some NCIPH staff came forward with warnings about working with RTI on this project because the development of a recent proposal had not gone well. NCIPH had gone into the partnership expecting to do most of the project only to be disappointed when the budget revealed that NCIPH would only be doing about 20% of the work. On further reflection, the NCIPH staff admitted that they had embarked on the project and then spent intensive hours working on the grant application without knowing how much of the project NCIPH would actually do. Thus, they advised asking RTI from the onset how much of the project NCIPH would actually do.

This story has a happy ending. When asked during the first telephone conversation, RTI staff explained that they wanted NCIPH to do about 80% of the project. Not only did RTI/NCIPH get selected for this national grant, but also all parties deemed the partnership successful. At the debriefing when the project ended, the comment was made that the distribution of work between the partners was close to the original estimate. How often do we jump at the chance to participate in a new community initiative without even asking a simple question about what—and how much—our role might be? In our haste to do good for the communities we serve, we oftentimes leave staff in the dark. Perhaps most telling from the RTI example is that staff indicated that they did not think it was their place to ask how much of the project NCIPH would be doing. They thought leadership should ask the question. Some mistakenly thought leadership had asked the question and that the understanding was that NCIPH would play a major role. Staff expects leadership to play that role of understanding scope, scale, and partners' roles. The most probable reason leaders may be reluctant to ask the question is that it may seem greedy or selfish to ask. But, it is not. It is businesslike and professional to want to understand the depth of the pool before you jump in with both feet.

False expectations lead to disappointment. But the dire consequence of disappointment is the unwillingness to work together again to partner on other initiatives. There is a value to tenured staff, but one of the liabilities is the memory of disappointment in relationships, which lingers and casts a pall over future opportunities. The simplest way to avoid this problem is for leadership to ask, "What was it that doomed that experience?" and "What can we do next time to make it better?"

Designing Governance

Clarity about governance versus management among all the partners is essential for a partnership to be sustainable. After all, every organization that is invited to the table has a primary mission, and every person has a "day job" that feeds his or her family. So what you are expecting is their engagement in a project that is tangential—but not central—to their being. This means that as the initiating partner, your job is to create an efficient way for the partners to meaningfully participate, to have a sense of ownership but not to be unnecessarily burdened.

Not-for-profit leaders are trained in understanding the role of governance as opposed to management, and a lack of clarity about the distinction will result in role confusion, micromanagement, and lack of strategic thinking. If the governing board starts managing, not only will it lead to confusion, stress, and discontent among staff who think management is their job, but also the governing board will then not be thinking strategically. In short, if the partners are managing the project, they have no time to do the hard job, which is to be strategic, policy oriented, and able to tackle the tough external issues such as securing resources. It is inevitable that if you take governing boards management information, they will manage, and as the lead partner, you want them to govern. When establishing a partnership, agreeing on how partners will govern the partnership is the foundation for the future. How is this done?

A partnership needs a mission and vision statement. This may seem trite, but the process of agreeing on words that describe who you are and where you are going will help build a consensus about identity. That statement should be created expeditiously and tersely and posted prominently. There is tremendous value in a crisp, clear mission and vision statement. One sentence, few words. NCIPH's mission statement reads, "Serving the state, leading the nation." That sums it up. We want to serve North Carolinians but in a way that lights the path for others in public health.

Perhaps more important is agreeing on outcomes or measures of success. Ask the partners, if we are really successful in five years, what will have happened? What are the concrete, visible outcomes that we can expect will spell success? A decade ago, a dozen of the leading children's hospitals got together to form BENCHmark,[1] a project to share outcome and performance data to determine best practices. At the first meeting at a central airport conference room, the organizations rapidly committed to participate, then hired the consultant (who was standing in the hall) and listened to and concurred with the consultant's approach and timeline for the project. The partnership was rapidly executed, and within two years, the partnership was receiving national acclaim and members were asked to speak and write about its success. The disconnect became apparent when the leaders who had been in that airport conference room were interviewed two years into the project. They had widely divergent ideas about whether the partnership had been successful because virtually no time had been spent reaching an agreement on the outcomes expected from the partnership. Thus, with a dozen different reasons for participating—for putting money on the table and spending hours collecting data—there were a dozen different ideas about what the final product was actually going to look like. Some had a Picasso in mind, others wanted a Rembrandt, and others a Chagall. Ultimately, there was a sense that the partnership had been a missed opportunity to shape the respective hospitals and the quality of care they delivered. Everyone agreed that the partnership had painted a picture, but the value was harshly debated because, after all, beauty is in the eye of the beholder.

Some of this disconnect is language. We talk about a partnership producing regular reports to the community but do not hold in our hands some sample reports or agree on a common format, length, style, and purpose. The word "report" conjures up different mental images about what that outcome will be and what it will accomplish. So being concrete in expected outcomes is essential. How much do we think diabetes will be reduced if we launch this initiative? By when? How will this be measured?

Early on, the way partners will govern the project must be established. Who will be the lead partner? How often will the partnership meet? What types of strategic information do the partners want to know? What decision-making process do they want to have? Five years ago, the Centers for Disease Control and Prevention, the Center for Creative Leadership, and the University of North Carolina's Kenan-Flagler Business School and School of Public Health began working together on the Public Health Leadership Institute (www.phli.org). From the inception of the partnership, monthly meetings were held with clear agendas around strategic issues of concern to the partners. Meanwhile, the director and a regular operations task force made management decisions. Over time, the partners' comfort with the direction of the partnership meant that meetings could be held bimonthly instead of monthly and could be shortened to an hour. In the process of sharing information and decision making, trust was built that enabled the partnership to not only govern this program effectively but also to strategize about leveraging this project to expand to provide other programs and services. And, after all, that is the ultimate outcome of a successful partnership, that the partners value one another's contribution, feel good about the accomplishment, and want to work together again to leverage their resources to improve community health.

Selecting the right partners, creating realistic expectations, and establishing a partnership governance structure are the key elements to successful partnership execution.

Reference

1.   Porter J. The benchmarking effort for networking children's hospitals (BENCHmark). *JCAHO J Qual Improv.* August 1995;21:395–406.

Chapter 15

Practicing Management and Leadership: Creating the Information Network for Public Health Officials

Edward L. Baker, Jr. and Janet E. Porter

W e will explore the principles described in the previous three chapters through illustrative case studies drawn from recent public health programs. By selecting cases and reflecting on lessons learned, we hope to illuminate some of the key critical success factors in developing new initiatives.

As we discuss these cases, we will not use individual names because we risk either overlooking someone who played a significant role or overemphasizing the value of another individual. In these discussions, we are not trying to recognize individual contributions, although these were significant, but rather to use the case to bring out points that may help you in the future. Nevertheless, the attentive reader will, no doubt, identify some of the key actors.

We begin with a somewhat chronological review of a companion set of initiatives designed to enhance the public health infrastructure through increased use of information technology. These initiatives were the Information Network for Public Health Officials (INPHO)[1] and the Health Alert Network (HAN). In this chapter, we will focus on the INPHO program.

Background

INPHO was initiated by the Centers for Disease Control and Prevention (CDC) in 1992 as part of its strategy to strengthen the infrastructure

Chapter Source: © 2005 Wolters Kluwer Health | Lippincott Williams & Wilkins. Originally published in *J Public Health Management Practice.* 2005; 11(5): 469–473.

of public health in the United States. The INPHO initiative addressed the serious national problem that public health professionals lacked ready access to much of the authoritative, technical information they needed to identify health dangers, implement prevention and health promotion strategies, and evaluate health program effectiveness. The INPHO promoted using state-of-the-art telecommunications and computer networks to give state and community public health practitioners new command over information resources. There were three essential components of the INPHO vision: linkage, information access, and data exchange. The INPHO computer networks and software linked local clinics, state and federal health agencies, hospitals, managed care organizations, and other providers, eliminating geographic and bureaucratic barriers to communication and information exchange. Through the INPHO initiative, public health practitioners were offered unprecedented electronic access to health publications, reports, databases, directories, and other information, thereby planting a seed for change and innovation. Electronic communications capacity enabled them to communicate and to exchange data locally and across the nation on the full universe of public health issues.[2]

Getting Started

The INPHO began with the idea that by giving public health practitioners computers, connecting the computers into networks, providing training, and making information accessible online, public health practice would be improved. The idea seems simple enough today, but that was in 1991–1992, when "Internet" was not a household word, and most public health agencies did not own a computer and often did not see why they should. At the CDC, pioneering work had been done to explore the use of computers to help analyze epidemiological information; programs such as WONDER and EpiInfo were under development to facilitate this application, and many elements of the INPHO vision were contained in previous work. However, only a relatively small number of local public health agencies benefited from these early innovations.

Context and Empowerment

In 1990, the CDC's newly appointed director articulated three priorities for the agency; the first was strengthening the public health infrastructure. The Institute of Medicine had issued a landmark report in 1988 entitled *The Future of Public Health*, which concluded that public health was in "disarray"[3] and something needed to be done about it. So, there were both a context for action and an empowering leader who articulated priorities within which the INPHO initiative could take root. The importance of support "from the top" cannot be overemphasized.

Let's say a bit more about empowerment. The CDC director did not spell out exactly what he wanted to happen and how he wanted it done. He empowered others to figure those things out, keep him informed of progress (and problems) and request advice and help when needed. In doing so, he enabled and empowered others to be creative in ways that he could never have imagined. It has repeatedly been our experience that by empowering others and creating an environment where risk taking and experimentation are encouraged, things happen that could not have been imagined. The key leadership task is creating an environment where people feel supported and protected to explore and be creative. Therefore, the INPHO emerged from an environment in which a priority was given to programs designed to strengthen the public health infrastructure, and the director empowered others to be innovative in addressing this priority. But, much more was needed to translate the idea into reality.

Communicating the Vision

A vision is something that you can see.

In the case of INPHO, a few pioneers saw the vision and understood the potential of advanced telecommunications technology and computer networks as essential tools for public health practice. But few others saw the potential and were able to "see" the vision. So, the next challenge was a communications challenge.

In *Leading Change*, John Kotter emphasizes that a vision must be communicated not just a few times but hundreds, even thousands of times, before it starts to take hold. Therefore, a vision must be clear and simple enough that it can be faithfully repeated. Never underestimate the importance of repetition in an organizational context. In fact, the best leaders are those who have the ability to say things the same way each time and also choose their words so that they are easily repeated. How often have you left a meeting with someone in authority and you turned to a coworker and asked, "Now what did he say?" Clarity and repeatability of the vision of a new project are crucial to building support and momentum for a new effort. In the case of INPHO, the vision was to provide public health officials with computers, with training in their use, with means to connect with others electronically, and with access to online information.

In addition to a clear vision, strategies must be articulated to guide action and program operations. Three core INPHO strategies flowed from the vision:

1. Connectivity
2. Information access
3. Data exchange

As it turned out, the first two strategies were much easier to implement than the third. In fact, methods of electronic data exchange remain major challenges today.

In the case of INPHO, there was also a good name. Never underestimate the value of a good name (and, in government, of a good acronym). People liked the name and really liked the acronym because the initiative was about enhancing access to information. So, choose your acronyms well.

Beyond the good name, there needed to be a way to visualize how the INPHO would actually work. It is impossible to get a program off the ground if you cannot explain what will happen and how things will work. Fortunately, a professor at a local university stressed the value of simulation, and since the INPHO was about using computers, it was natural to use a computer-based simulation to illustrate how the system would work. Recall that this was happening before e-mail and the Internet.

The simulation tool was used as part of the process of selling the idea to decision makers and potential funders. This relationship-based selling required a clear presentation and a well-articulated business case (both of which will be discussed in later chapters).

At this juncture, INPHO planners had a supportive environment, a vision, a set of core strategies, a simple and repeatable name, and a simulation of how INPHO would work. But, much more needed to happen before the idea became reality.

The Zealots

A small group of thoughtful people can change the world. Indeed, it is the only thing that ever has.

—Margaret Mead

In the case of the INPHO initiative, a small band of pioneers (the "zealots") inspired one another, fostered mutual creativity, and provided exceptional amounts of positive energy that allowed the vision to stay alive and ultimately become reality. There is no substitute for optimism and positive energy in the development of a new initiative. Pessimists can play a useful role in some aspects of organizational life, but rarely in the startup of a new initiative. Starting something new is hard work; pessimists can make it much harder. Do you remember our discussion of "derailers" in Chapter 14? A band of zealots will get you much farther and with more fun. Look carefully at new initiatives with which you are familiar. Can you see the zealots? What about Microsoft or Apple—do you see any zealots there?

Among the zealots was one who stood out as an exceptional collaborator and who became the leader of the INPHO initiative. In previous chapters, we have stressed some of the characteristics that make good partnerships work: humility, sharing risks and rewards, building trust, and quality leadership. The leader of INPHO exemplified these and other outstanding qualities that made people simply want to work with him.

In many respects, this person embodied the principles of servant leadership ably described by Robert Greenleaf as one who wants to serve first and makes the conscious choice to be a leader second.[5] Without this charismatic and committed leader, the INPHO project would never have gotten off the ground.

Mobilizing Resources

If you want to build something, you need resources. In this and in many other successful initiatives, it was important to try to identify support, crystallize the vision, and identify a small group of people actually to begin the work *before* seeking resources to do the job. In an organizational setting, you should get "top-down" support, have a clear and compelling vision of the goal with tools to help visualize the goal, and identify the nucleus of your team before seeking resources.

In the INPHO initiative, two important things happened that helped garner resources to fund the program. These happened in the same time frame and for different reasons, and both rest on the principle that "relationships are everything, all else is derivative." As a government agency, the CDC funding derives from the appropriations process. In that regard, members of Congress and their staffs are regularly seeking new ways to provide benefits to their constituents and to support programs that are good for the nation. Ideally, from the perspective of the appropriations process, new programs have the greatest chance of success if there is demonstrable local benefit as well as a pressing national need. In the case of INPHO, both criteria were met and, through a series of conversations enabled by strong existing relationships, funding was made available to launch INPHO demonstration projects in several states. A second line of support was developed in Georgia through a large foundation that was interested in making Georgia the "flagship" of the INPHO initiative. In the case of the foundation, as was the case with the federal appropriations process, local benefit and national need were critical to gaining the generous support of the foundation.

Initial Deployment of Resources—The "Low-Hanging Fruit" and Tight Management

With resources in hand, the INPHO team set out to implement the vision. The team was looking for some "low-hanging fruit"—projects that were ripe for implementation and relatively easy to execute. In the early phases of project implementation, it is best to do a few relatively easy things first, thereby demonstrating results and giving a sense of accomplishment to the team and partners. Also, in view of the substantial funding commitment from the Georgia foundation and the lack of understanding of the INPHO within the CDC, it was essential that value be demonstrated close to home. So, the team decided to identify some early success possibilities. Ultimately, the team made CDC's *Morbidity and Mortality Weekly Report (MMWR)* available online, created a model program in a local health agency in a remote area of south Georgia, and structured a visit to the south Georgia site to demonstrate the value of INPHO to the funding foundation. By making the *MMWR* available online, CDC leaders came to recognize the potential of information technology as a means to disseminate information, well before Web sites became commonplace. So, the lesson of early action is that you should find a few things that are relatively easy and "close to home" early in the course of the project to demonstrate success and the value of the project. In the remote south Georgia health department, the use of a new tool called "e-mail" created a major stir because it provided connectivity in ways never experienced before.

Tight project management was essential to the success of the early phase of the INPHO project in Georgia. With a handpicked team, early project activities followed a carefully constructed timetable. The first year of the project went exactly on time and within budget, demonstrating that the INPHO team was a reliable partner. Being a reliable partner is something that is demonstrated over time. Trust comes from having accomplished something together.

Taking the Program to Scale

After some initial successes and the usual growing pains associated with any new venture, the INPHO program reached out to 12 states across the nation, providing modest levels of support for innovative use of information systems in public health programs. The funding was a valuable catalyst for change. At this stage, few standards existed, so the programs were encouraged to be innovative and flexible in their approach. National conferences were held to bring together these innovators and stimulate the sharing of ideas and opportunities. This stage of growth and expansion was characterized by the development of new applications for existing needs. For example, some states used the INPHO support to develop their first Web site. In other settings, e-mail networks were developed, and online information resources were made available. Extensive staff training was central to the success of the INPHO. If we have one major message related to taking the program to scale, it is the need for training. Just as you must "strain to communicate" in sharing the vision early in the course of a new project, a complete commitment to training is essential to the success of early implementation of the vision.

As part of the process of taking the INPHO initiative to scale, a network of pioneers emerged across the country in support of the vision. These individuals led efforts in their own states and provided support and encouragement to colleagues across the nation. Fostering this group of colleagues was essential to the ongoing success of the INPHO program. As you develop your own programs, be sure to nurture these informal "communities of practice," a concept that has gained much recent attention as vital to the diffusion of innovation.

Laying the Foundation for the Future

The INPHO program served a crucial role in demonstrating the value of empowering local public health practitioners with information technology and in developing communities of practice across the nation. The foundation was laid for other information technology initiatives, such as the Health Alert Network and the Public Health Information

Network. For these and other related initiatives, the INPHO program pioneered the way with the use of information technology throughout the public health system, thereby supporting the priority articulated by the CDC director in 1990 of strengthening the public health infrastructure.

Lessons Learned

As we look back and reflect on what factors contributed to the success of the INPHO program, there were several critical success factors:

1. Support from top leadership and a context for action
2. An environment that encouraged risk taking
3. A clear, compelling vision that was easily communicated
4. A computer-based simulation to aid communication
5. A band of "zealots" committed to the vision
6. A trusted leader skilled in partnership development
7. Resource mobilization based on strong existing partnerships
8. Early demonstration of value close to home through tight management
9. Program implementation through flexible approaches
10. Creation of communities of practice to foster innovation

As you create new initiatives, we hope that some of these lessons may be valuable, and we hope this story of the INPHO initiative has been interesting.

References

1. Baker EL, Ross D. Information and surveillance systems and community health: building the public health information infrastructure. *J Public Health Manage Pract.* 1996;2(4):58–60.
2. National Health Information Center and Health Information Resource Database. Information Network for Public Health Officials. Available at: http://www.health.gov/NHIC/NHICScripts/Entry.cfm?HRCode=HR2686. Accessed June 1, 2005.
3. The Institute of Medicine. *The Future of Public Health.* Washington: National Academy Press; 1988: xi.
4. Kotter JP. *Leading Change.* Boston, MA: Harvard Business School Press; 1996.
5. Greenleaf RK. *On Becoming a Servant Leader.* San Francisco, CA. Jossey-Bass Publishers; 1996.

Chapter 16

The Health Alert Network: Partnerships, Politics, and Preparedness

Edward L. Baker, Jr. and Janet E. Porter

Building on Chapter 15, which applied previous chapters' messages to the development of the Information Network for Public Health Officials (INPHO), we would like to share lessons learned from a later program, the Health Alert Network (HAN). In this case, the value of partnerships will be highlighted along with insights into the politics of funding for public health practice. Finally, we will relate the HAN to the overall theme of public health preparedness.

The Health Alert Network Vision

In keeping with the vision of INPHO described in our previous chapter, the purpose of the HAN was to create an information network, such that every local health agency would be connected electronically and be able to use information technology to support its mission. The initial emphasis was on "network," not on the "alert" part of the name. As you will see, "alerting" became a central and highly visible feature following September 11, 2001.

Chapter Source: © 2005 Wolters Kluwer Health | Lippincott Williams & Wilkins. Originally published in *J Public Health Management Practice.* 2005; 11(6): 574–576.

Getting Started: The NACCHO Partnership

In the mid- to late-1990s, the National Association of County and City Health Officials (NACCHO) experienced growth on its way to becoming a major national force in public health practice. As part of its annual planning conference, the NACCHO leadership decided to become more active in advocacy and to focus its advocacy on two priorities: training and information system development. Without the active involvement of NACCHO working at the national level, the HAN would never have become a reality.

Much effort had been invested by the Public Health Practice Program Office (PHPPO) of the Centers for Disease Control and Prevention (CDC) in strengthening NACCHO as an organization through the late 1980s and early 1990s. This commitment to the growth of NACCHO by PHPPO resulted in a continuously expanding relationship, which provided the foundation of the HAN program. Establishing a strong foundational relationship before initiating program development discussions is often bypassed in the haste to "get to work." We learned from this initiative that relationship development, with attendant enhancement of trust and understanding, was central to the success of the HAN program and was a precondition for its success.

Working within the Political Process

Once the NACCHO leadership decided to adopt advocacy as a priority, the organization set forth to establish itself as a force in Washington, D.C. The most important first step in that journey was hiring an experienced former senior congressional staff employee who understood the workings of Congress, particularly the appropriations process. Her wisdom, coupled with her strategic insights and tactical skills, enabled the process to obtain extraordinary attention on Capitol Hill and, subsequently, substantial funding. Coincidentally, she had also helped to secure funding for the INPHO program several years earlier.

Around the same time, another congressional staff member, who had a public health background, learned of the CDC's interest in strengthening the public health infrastructure and particularly in providing information technology as a tool to improve local and state public health agencies. She also made a key connection between the need for a strong infrastructure and growing fears in Congress related to bioterrorism.

"Funding follows fear" is a maxim that has characterized the way our political system has addressed public health threats for decades. For example, the CDC Epidemic Intelligence Service (EIS) was funded in the 1950s in response to fears of biological warfare. In the case of the HAN, we decided, before September 11, 2001, to link our case for funding to early efforts to fund terrorism preparedness.

Making the Case, Creating the Name

Through the efforts of NACCHO, a report was requested by the Senate Appropriations Committee (a tactic often used to establish the case for a new funding initiative). In the course of developing the report, a senior PHPPO staff member coined the name "Health Alert Network." The name was vitally important in that it accurately described the program and served as a succinct label to use in lobbying for funding. Furthermore, by being asked to write a report justifying the HAN, the CDC team was forced to articulate needs, opportunities, challenges, and approaches. Developing a case statement for any new initiative can be a valuable way to crystallize the vision and help mobilize support.

Building the Network, Defining Success

As part of the initial phase of implementation, a dedicated team was assembled[1] and, as part of the initial planning, created definitions of success with respect to building the network. The team developed an operational definition of what it meant to be connected to the network (e.g., continuous high-speed Internet access). Today, many of us have continuous high-speed Internet access in our homes; in 1999, at the start of the HAN initiative, most health agencies did not have this capacity, and many did not think they even needed it. By defining success in operational terms, the HAN team provided leadership and established a key success parameter, which was maintained over time. Then, major technical assistance and cooperative agreement funding was put in place, which allowed the "construction" of the HAN. At that time (1999–2000), the focus was on network development. On one occasion, the system was "tested" with an "alert" to explore the ability to transmit a message over the network.

Responding to Terrorism and Urgent Health Threats

On September 11, 2001, the HAN was to send its first alert message to public health leaders. Had the groundwork not been laid in previous years, this vital communication infrastructure would not have been in place. The foresight and concerted effort that preceded September 11 allowed the system to be used when it mattered; in many respects, the public health system had been prepared through strategic partnerships and focused technical capacity building. Subsequently, the HAN has been used hundreds of times for national notifications following the anthrax attacks, during West Nile fever outbreaks, and for other emergencies. Furthermore, enhanced federal funding allowed for greater expansion of the HAN such that all local health agencies are now connected to the network.

Developing Local and State Health Alert Networks, Sustaining the Vision

Although the HAN was originally conceived of as a national system, state and local HANs have been developed. The HAN vision has become part of the fabric of public health practice. In North Carolina, for example, the state's HAN is used regularly to notify practitioners of infectious disease outbreaks and public health implications of national disasters, such as hurricanes. Today, the sustainability of the HAN is ensured as a result of the clear demonstration of ongoing value to public health practitioners.

Summary

The extraordinary success of the HAN initiative was based on a number of factors. First, a strong, preexisting partnership with NACCHO enabled development of a shared vision. Second, advocacy, guided by an experienced former congressional staff member, was essential in building political support, with attendant resources to build the network. Third, defining success in operational terms and providing technical assistance and funding to achieve success were essential in bringing the vision to reality and for preparing to use the HAN. Fourth, using the HAN following September 11 and during the anthrax threats demonstrated the value of investing in the public health infrastructure and helped to secure additional funding. Finally, institutionalization of HANs across the nation at the state and local level has ensured that the HAN vision will be sustained for decades to come.

Reference

1.   O'Carroll PW, Yasnoff WA, Ward ME, Ripp LH, Martin EL, eds. *Public Health Informatics and Information Systems*. New York, NY: Springer-Verlag; 2003.

Managing
Communication

Chapter 17

Meetings, Meetings, and More Meetings

Janet E. Porter and Edward L. Baker, Jr.

Managers spend the majority of their time in meetings. One of the greatest challenges of busy managers is to control their daily calendar so that they can squeeze in as many meetings as possible. Indeed, it often seems that you cannot get anything done because of all the meetings all day long. Meetings are often seen as an impediment to getting work done rather than the means to get work done. The successful manager must be able to organize, lead, and participate effectively in meetings to advance the organization's objectives. So, what is the secret to effective meetings? The principles of effective meetings are the same whether it is a fairly routine, decision-making meeting or a large, strategic meeting. Here we will discuss the critical competency of organizing and conducting effective meetings for managers.

Conducting Effective Meetings

First, the manager needs to ask whether a meeting is really the best means to get the work done. Many times meetings get scheduled without any clear purpose. We may schedule a meeting to avoid actually making a challenging decision or providing tough feedback. How many

Chapter Source: © 2006 Lippincott Williams & Wilkins, Inc. Originally published in J Public Health Management Practice. 2006; 12(1): 103–106.

times have you heard in response to what is going to be done, "We'll schedule a meeting," as if the meeting were an outcome in and of itself? So, the first question to ask yourself before scheduling a meeting is whether a meeting is necessary. Could you just send an e-mail or make a phone call or write a memo? Or, could you just make a decision and announce it? Do not use meetings as an excuse to delay making a decision or taking action.

Once you have decided a meeting really is necessary, ask yourself, What is the purpose of the meeting? The purpose of a meeting can be to inform, seek feedback, answer questions, organize, problem solve, negotiate, or make a decision. Knowing why you have called a meeting and what constitutes success is essential. Every aspect of a meeting, from the invite list to the room location to the agenda to the length of the meeting, should be driven by a clear sense of the meeting's purpose. When working through the specifics of an all-day meeting for a public health agency, the health director and his staff were asked what the purpose of the meeting was. After 30 minutes of debate, it became clear that there was no consensus on why almost 30 people from the agency were planning to spend the majority of the day together. If the purpose is not clear to the organizers, it is unlikely to be clear to the participants. There is nothing more frustrating than leaving a long meeting and wondering, as you exit, what the meeting was all about. Ask yourself: When the meeting is over and we are thrilled with the success of the meeting, what will have happened? What constitutes a home run? The best way to have clarity about a meeting's purpose is actually to write down what constitutes success. Doing this keeps everyone focused on the big picture. For example, you might note, "A good decision will be made whether to continue this program."

Top 10 Secrets to Having an Effective Meeting

1. Have a clear purpose.
2. Invite the right people.
3. Arrange a convenient location and an appropriate room.
4. Schedule only the amount of time that you really need.
5. Organize the agenda to meet the meeting's purpose.
6. Distribute key documents in advance.
7. Conduct the meeting to keep it on schedule and on task.
8. State the purpose of the meeting at the beginning.
9. Summarize the meeting and explain the next steps.
10. Keep and distribute minutes.

The tendency is to inform participants about the meeting's topic but not about the meeting's purpose. Topic and purpose are not the same. For example, knowing that the topic of a meeting is to discuss the Women, Infants, and Children program is not the same thing as understanding that the purpose of the meeting is to finalize a communication plan for recipients of the Women, Infants, and Children program. Thus, when sending an announcement for a meeting, remember to explain the purpose of the meeting.

A few years ago, we had a meeting scheduled with four partners on a project to decide on whether to continue to invest in developing and marketing a new leadership program. We were very clear that the objective of the meeting was to make a firm decision. The goal was not to persuade all the partners to proceed or to drop the new leadership program—just to get them to reach consensus on whether to proceed. With that clarity of purpose, the meeting was a big success in that the partners made a decision—in this case to cancel the program. Furthermore, in the intervening years, the decision has not been rethought; subsequent developments have proved that the partners made a wise decision.

At the North Carolina Institute for Public Health (NCIPH), we routinely schedule briefing meetings a week before an educational retreat or conference to review logistics: Who is going to handle the introductions? What readings or cases or books did each instructor want the participants to read? Who is going to explain the evaluation? The clear purpose of this type of meeting is to organize and inform. The agenda for the upcoming retreat is always distributed to everyone so that staff members involved in the retreat understand their respective roles every day.

We also schedule two debriefings following every conference. The first debriefing happens as the participants are walking out the door. At that point, the purpose of the debriefing is to review the logistics, to find out what aspects went particularly well or need to be changed for the next time. A second debriefing occurs a few weeks later once we have evaluation results from the participants. For this latter debriefing, the focus is on the curriculum content and speaker comments, and whether educational objectives are being met. Program aspects such as sequencing and timing of the speakers and courses are the focus. Organizations holding routine meetings with a clear purpose can assure consistency and quality of services while advancing learning about best practices.

Third, the logistics of a meeting should be determined solely on the basis of what the meeting is intended to accomplish. Think about who should attend, where the meeting should be held, and what should be the length of the meeting. Managers typically consider who should attend a meeting but spend much less time focusing on site or length. The only thought given to location is whether the room is convenient or of appropriate size. For most meetings, these considerations are certainly enough. However, for significant meetings, the room arrangement must support the meeting's purpose. There is nothing worse than arriving for a meeting with a room setup that does not work at all. At the American Public Health Association meeting a few years ago, a small national organization called its annual meeting for members. Participants arrived to find themselves in a room set up classroom style. With one small conference table at the front of the room, those arriving first huddled around the conference table, with stragglers arriving trying to pull up to the group. Those responsible for the meeting arrived late and did not bring agendas. Needless to say, the meeting not only did not accomplish the purpose but also left a lasting negative impression on participants.

Then there is the matter of a meeting's length. Too often, meetings are routinely scheduled for an hour when 15 minutes would suffice. Dr Bill Roper, the former Centers for Disease Control and Prevention director, when speaking to the Public Health Leadership Institute scholars about the importance of time management, advocated for 15-minute meetings. He noted that shortening the time expectation of a meeting focuses participants on the task at hand and provides clarity of purpose. Afterward, some commented on how infeasible this seemed. Maybe having 15-minute meetings seems awfully short, but would not 30 minutes often work? Challenge yourself not to think about meetings in 1-hour increments, and you could find a lot more time in your days.

Of course, using participants' precious time wisely should be a factor when considering a meeting's length. Preparing materials for distribution and reading prior to the meeting is one means to limit the meeting's length. It is common to be thoughtful about participants' time when they are volunteers or senior leaders in a community. For this type of participant you might distribute an agenda item with related materials in advance, for example. However, just as much thought should be given to internal meetings, as staff time is equally precious. It should be part of the culture to come well prepared to meetings and to be on time. Managers should model that behavior by organizing meetings thoughtfully and coming well prepared themselves.

Now we get to organizing the agenda for the meeting. Of course, for many it would be a step forward to have an agenda at all. Every meeting agenda should start and end the same way. The first item on the agenda should always be the meeting's purpose. And the last item should always be a summary of the meeting and a statement of the next steps. The principles of primacy and recency apply to meetings. What these basic psychological principles mean is that people will remember the first few minutes of a meeting and the last few minutes. We do not tend to remember much in between—unless, of course, there is an altercation or controversy. Thus, make the first and last items the clearest portions of the meeting. Artful agenda management means thinking through what the topics will be, how much time will be spent on each topic, the sequence of the topics, and who will present or lead each topic.

Right after introducing the purpose of the meeting, the next agenda item for major meetings is to review and approve the minutes. Meetings are a vital tool in project management. Keeping track of what happens in those meetings is an important aspect of moving a project along by recording decisions, commitments, and project progress. The secret to keeping good minutes is to prepare them immediately after the meeting—when the discussion is still fresh in your mind. Recall decays over time, and it becomes difficult to remember what happened and what was decided even a few days afterward.

Naturally, the items on a meeting's agenda should be in a logical sequence—building upon one another. A common mistake is to try to accomplish too much in some meetings, and then time management becomes a problem. When you call a meeting for discussion and participative decision making, you must schedule adequate time for that processing by the participants. If it seems before a meeting that there is too much on the agenda, there is. Review all agenda items and remove those that are not central to the agency's goals.

Ideally, a relationship should exist between a public health agency's strategic goals for the year and meeting topics. We once had a public health agency ask for help because it was not making progress toward its goals. It was easy to see why. When agendas for its major meetings were reviewed, it was clear that the agency was spending all its time on daily operational issues but no time on strategic issues or goals. There was no apparent relationship between how the leadership and staff were spending their time together in meetings and what they had committed to accomplish in their strategic goals. One organization in Texas arranged agendas for all their major meetings around its strategic goals. Nothing was placed on an agenda unless it supported a strategic goal for the organization.

Time is the major resource managers deploy. If the time spent in meetings is used for nonimportant items, then the manager is literally spending the agency's resources unwisely. It is no different from purchasing supplies frivolously.

At NCIPH, we keep a "We Would Be Proud" list prominently displayed. The staff write the list on the basis of what they want to accomplish in the next year. We try to revisit the list to recognize and celebrate the key accomplishments. This year we had staff sign up or autograph the list as a public display of commitment to the goals.

So, it is the time for the meeting, the right participants are in attendance, they have been sent relevant materials in advance, and you have copies of the agenda in front of everyone. Now it is up to the skillful manager to conduct the meeting to accomplish the original purpose. First, make sure introductions are made. Second, clarify the purpose of the meeting. Answer any questions about the meeting's purpose. Then the trick is to manage the meeting so that all the agenda items are discussed and decisions made. Skillful facilitators of meetings make sure discussions are balanced, the meeting moves along, and attention is focused on the overall goal of the meeting. One manager was notorious for scheduling three or four major agenda items for a meeting and never getting to the last items because he did not keep the meeting moving along. Putting an item on the agenda is really a form of a commitment between the meeting's organizer and the participants. It is an implicit agreement that the participants will get to all the items on the agenda. If you view each agenda item as a promise, a sort of contract with the participants that all those items will be discussed, then you are more likely to assure that everything on the agenda gets a fair hearing.

Finally, the skillful facilitator summarizes what has been discussed and explains next steps. The most common mistake made in meeting management is to fail to allow for enough time to summarize and conclude the meeting. Recapping what has just happened in the meeting and restating the meeting's purpose and decisions is the role of the meeting's organizer.

Summary

Being able to organize and conduct meetings effectively just may be the most important competency of all. After all, how you spend your days adds up to how you spend your years. And how you spend your hours every day is oftentimes in meetings. It is up to leaders and managers to make sure that time is well spent.

For more information about the NCIPH, go to http://www.sph.unc.edu/nciph.

Chapter 18

Improving Your Presentation Skills

Janet E. Porter and Dianne Cerce

"Can you speak?" It is that proverbial request to come and present on a specific topic—to the county commissioners, to a local not-for-profit, to a potential partner—that strikes terror in some public health managers' hearts. Every time a survey of people's greatest fears is conducted, it seems that giving a speech ranks right up there, higher than fear of heights or even death. But learning public speaking skills is no different from learning skills for whipping up a great meal or having a great golf swing—it is really all about practice. Governor Sarah Palin was all over the news when we began this chapter because she had just given a show-stopping speech to the National Republican Convention. Meanwhile, Barack Obama's oratorical skills undoubtedly contributed to his successful bid to be our new president. Neither of them woke up one day with that ability. The more you speak in front of groups, the more comfortable and effective you will be. It also helps to have tips from the pros on preparing and delivering and evaluating a great speech. So let's begin at the beginning.

The Request to Speak

Every speaker can give an example of when he or she really misread the audience. This lapse can be everything from not knowing who the audience is, to not knowing how large the audience will be, to not understanding the audience's expectations for the presentation. So it all

123

starts with the request. The first thing to do is to figure out whether this is a good use of your time. Here are the questions to ask:

- What does the person who invited you to speak want you to accomplish?
- Who is the audience? What is their professional background? How many will be in the audience?
- What is your educational objective? What do you want them to learn or understand?
- How much time is allotted for the speech? How much time for presentation versus questions and answers?
- How formal or informal do you want this presentation to be? PowerPoint slides? Handouts?

One thing the answers to these questions will determine is whether you are the best person to fulfill this speaking request. Do not hesitate to recommend someone else if that person would be more qualified to address the topic. However, do not do that just because you don't feel comfortable in front of groups. Being in a key leadership role means you have to be able to get in front of groups and effectively communicate.

Susan, a new county public health director, failed to ask these questions for her first speaking engagement to a community group. She arrived at the presentation only to discover that only 10 people were in attendance, she waited over 90 minutes because they were running behind schedule, and she wasn't technically qualified to answer some of their specific questions, which were about restaurant and food-handling inspections. She realized afterward that the presentation had been a waste of her time and that she had staff in the health department who would have been better qualified to answer their questions.

If you decide you are the best person to fulfill the request to speak, make sure you understand what is being asked of you. This step is especially important when you've never spoken at a particular venue before or when you are new to your position. When you are new, you may get many requests to speak. People want to get to know you. They want to be able to hear you speak, to decide whether you sound authentic, whether they are going to like you, and so on. When Fred assumed a new role in public health, he was swamped with requests—in one week, he reported doing seven presentations. Now, some of these presentations were the same remarks, but still, getting in front of all those groups can be a bit overwhelming—even for an extrovert. With few exceptions, all of his presentations went fine, until he presented at the annual meeting of the Society for the Prevention of Cruelty to Animals (SPCA). He hadn't asked the right questions and assumed they just wanted a few remarks when what they really wanted was a keynote address. The planners were remarkably forgiving when he sat down after just a few minutes, even though the agenda allotted 25 minutes for him to speak.

It is important to make sure you understand not only your part of the program but also who is speaking before and after you. Obtain a copy of the entire agenda for the meeting. If you can, make sure that your presentation is appropriately placed on the agenda. For example, you may want to request a change in the agenda if your talk follows a speaker making a controversial argument. That speaker may put everyone in a no-nonsense mood, leaving you with a contrarian audience. Or, if you wish to raise a serious issue you may not want to follow a light-hearted presentation that gets everyone laughing.

Also, make sure in advance that the room is set up for an effective delivery of your presentation. The following is a simple checklist for ensuring that everything will go well.

- Specify the room setup. Nothing is worse than expecting to have people talk in small groups only to walk in and discover that the room is set up auditorium style, making the small-group interaction impossible.
- Order the appropriate audiovisual equipment. Do you want a flip chart or a screen? Don't assume anything will be there.
- Check the room and practice with the audiovisual equipment, if possible. Ideally you would visit the room in advance, run through the presentation, and really understand how the laser pointer or the remote works.
- Proofread and edit your slides and handouts, and print the right number of handouts for the estimated audience.

Planning Your Remarks

What is your message? Write it down in one or two sentences. Your basic goal in delivering this message should be to tell the audience what you want to say, then say it, then tell them what you just said. The more clarity you have, the easier it will be to prepare your remarks. For most audiences, it is safe to assume that they are similar to your neighbors—they are intelligent but don't know what you really do or what public health is really all about. So, beginning with an explanation of where you're coming from is often good. If you're there to ask for something, explain as plainly as possible what the need is and what they can do to help meet that need. What is the most effective way to get your message across? Oftentimes, show-and-tell works really well. Don't limit yourself to PowerPoint slides or handouts, however; use charts, video clips, or demonstrations—anything that illustrates your message.

The following is a typical outline of a presentation:

- **Introduction:** Use your introduction to establish credibility with the audience and establish interest. Tell a story that illustrates the need and grabs the audience's attention. This is the point where you unveil your message in one or two sentences that frame the entire presentation and convince the audience that this topic is important. The previous chapter mentioned the basic psychological rule of recency and primacy: people remember the first few minutes and the last few minutes of any experience. A classic example is that staff remembers their first day of work and their last day of work. Presentations are like that too. If you don't grab the audience at the beginning, it is hard to engage them at all. So spend time developing a catchy introduction.

- **Objectives:** Tell the audience the purpose of your presentation. Be clear about what you are asking for or educating them about. It is easy to lose an audience in a mere five minutes if they have no idea why you are there. If you want them to learn something, tell them what you want them to learn. If you are seeking their approval, explain clearly what you want them to approve of.

- **Agenda:** Give the audience an outline of your remarks.

- **Content:** The most important thing about the body of your talk is that your audience be able to understand it. Be clear and concise, construct your thoughts logically, and don't bury your message. When a famous author was asked why he wrote such a long letter, he indicated he didn't have time to write a short one. It is often difficult to synthesize and boil down the message when it is a big, complicated, multifaceted issue with many different opinions on the resolution. Explain the complexities, but always keep the main points clear, and hit them hard throughout your talk. Avoid acronyms. You will lose your audience if they do not understand what you are talking about because you are using jargon.

- **Conclusion:** At the end of your presentation, drive home your message. In the introduction, you told the audience what you were going to tell them. Now it is time to tell them again, emphasizing the key points that you want them to remember.

■ **Questions and Answers:** The question-and-answer period gives you a chance either to establish or lose your credibility. To prepare, anticipate what the top 10 questions will be. Write down those questions and their answers. Then prepare the answers in your PowerPoint slides or in handouts. It is very impressive for a speaker to conclude and then when asked the first question, answer, "I am glad you asked that" and flip to the next slide illustrating the answer. Audience members are wowed by that, thinking, "Boy this person is well prepared."

Key Elements of an Effective Presentation

You probably have heard some speakers you will never forget. A few years ago, former Secretary of State Colin Powell gave a speech in Ohio to the Columbus Speech and Hearing Foundation. His wife, Alma, is an audiologist, and Colin Powell began his remarks by telling an amusing story about Alma inviting him up to her apartment after a few dates, which got him thinking lustful thoughts. He went eagerly, only to discover that what she really wanted was to test his hearing because she was convinced he had hearing loss, and in fact, those years in the infantry had impaired his hearing. Needless to say, he had the audience—many of whom were audiologists—eating out the palm of his hand with this personal story that also touched on their reason for being there. An effective presentation is **interesting** from the very beginning. Sometimes it is humor that grabs an audience, sometimes it is a powerful personal story, which, as in this case, connects back to the presentation's topic. The key is to create interest in your audience.

President Jimmy Carter has that incredible ability to make it seem that he is talking directly to you. He is passionate about reducing the economic disparities in this country. When he speaks, he engages the audience immediately. He asks them, "Do you know a poor person? Are you friends with someone who is homeless, who has never owned a car, who is on welfare? If you don't really know anyone who is poor, how can you begin to think that you will implement good policies on behalf of the poor?" He goes right to the heart of the matter and right to the heart of his audience. What will you do to make sure that the group takes a personal interest in your remarks? An effective presentation is **meaningful** to the audience, it is relevant. The topic is connected to their lives. So you have to connect the topic to the members of the audience.

Finally, you have to be **believable**. How will you establish credibility with your audience? Always give whoever is introducing you a brief biography of your relevant personal and professional accomplishments. Tell them exactly what you would like them to say. They should introduce you in a way that establishes your credibility with the audience. For 10 years at the University of North Carolina, we have held the Management Academy of Public Health. We discovered that the evaluation results could be tied directly to whether the speakers were introduced. Even with a mere five-sentence introduction that demonstrated the faculty member's credibility—their public health experience, that they had authored a book or consulted for the Centers for Disease Control and Prevention—evaluations would be higher. Beyond your biographical information, believability is also based upon authenticity. To be authentic, you need to speak from the heart. Reading from notes does not convey that you are knowledgeable about your topic or that they are actually your words. So, knowing the material enough that you can appear to talk extemporaneously is important. A lot of speakers today use PowerPoint slides to help track the major points—as a substitute for notes. Use whatever tools help you to keep track of your remarks without reading.

Measures of Success

One key measure of success is that you are memorable. I once saw James Carville on a book tour with his wife, Mary Matalin, promoting their book *All's Fair: Love, War, and Running for President*. He gave a five-minute speech, which, 16 years later, I can recite word for word. His speech delivered a powerful message about what he, an ardent Democrat who had just led Clinton's successful bid for the White House, and Mary, a powerful Republican who had led Bush's unsuccessful reelection campaign, had in common. He told poignant stories, conveying that what they had in common was the desire to leave this country a better place. If people can remember your message a few weeks later, that is a base hit—years later is a grand slam.

The second measure of success is that you convince the audience to agree with you. By and large, you are trying to sell an idea. So if you have persuaded the audience to think as you do about your idea, you have been successful.

Finally, and most importantly, your speech has been successful if you have accomplished your objective. It is easy to lose sight of your objective. Did you set out to solicit their support for a new program for fighting diabetes in children? You may have entertained them with a touching story or even informed them about the issue of how diabetes is affecting our society, but if you haven't informed them about your program and obtained their support, you have not met your objective.

A very important reason to give presentations is to develop the relationships that will further your public health organization's goals down the road. Barbara Sabol, a program officer with the Kellogg Foundation, always says that relationships are primary, and everything else is secondary. So, what you are largely doing when you speak—either within a health department or organization, or externally with key partners—is building relationships. The worst professional meeting and presentation I ever had in my career involved a grilling from grant sponsors—with Sabol from the Kellogg Foundation, Dr. Ed Baker and Dr. Bill Roper from the CDC, and other key public health leaders in the room. We thought our presentation was a pure disaster, particularly when they mentioned discontinuing the grant funding. We couldn't decide whether to crawl under the table or throw spitballs. However, afterward we worked even harder to make the project better and were able to build trust and respect with the sponsors. When we look back, we see that experience as pivotal to the success of the project because the sponsors set a high bar for our performance, and being able to jump over that bar strengthened our position in the long run. So don't lose sight that a measure of success may be what happens after the presentation. No matter what the outcome of the presentation itself, true success might mean that you have laid a foundation for working together to improve health, which, of course, is the ultimate goal.

Chapter 19

Managing in the Information Age: Preventing "Electronic Fatigue Syndrome"

Edward L. Baker, Jr. and Stephen N. Orton

Quite some time ago, as voicemail began to play a role in our work lives, a former director of the National Institute for Occupational Safety and Health (NIOSH) provided a wonderful insight. Drawing on the workplace distinction between "self-paced" work and "machine-paced" work,[1] he referred to the advent of voicemail as "machine-paced work for executives." By this he meant that the pace of work was beginning to be influenced by the use of a particular form of information technology. Implicit in this characterization was the understanding that this new technology carried with it a risk of causing or contributing to occupational stress, as was the case with other types of machine-paced work, for example, the assembly line.

E-mail Mania

Just as voicemail represented a means of improving the efficiency of information exchange, so we are now faced with a more complex array of information technologies designed to enhance productivity and speed information flow. E-mail has now become the most visible sign of machine-paced work for executives and a recent computer "killer application." Everyone has to have it, and it has changed the work paradigm. E-mail represents a huge productivity multiplier, virtually

Chapter Source: © 2006 Wolters Kluwer Health | Lippincott Williams & Wilkins. Originally published in *J Public Health Management Practice.* 2006; 12(3): 298–300.

eliminating time and distance as barriers and allowing highly efficient, asynchronous communication between individuals and across groups.

The downside is that someone has to read all that e-mail. The time we spend sending and receiving e-mails has become a significant part of each workday. For example, a 1999 internal survey conducted by the Intel Corporation revealed that approximately three million e-mail messages per day were sent or received by Intel employees. The average worker's in-box contained 200 messages and approximately 2.5 hours per day were spent managing e-mail. To address this challenge, Intel started an e-mail training program to create a more efficient e-mail culture.[2]

E-mail usage now "paces" our day by creating the expectation for rapid response to messages. How often has someone asked you, "Did you get my e-mail?" This expectation creates a culture of checking e-mail to see whether "something important" has arrived—a particularly challenging issue for those of us on the obsessive compulsive side (which many managers and leaders tend to be). A July 2001 Gallup Organization survey showed that 51% of workers checked e-mail every hour while 32% checked it continuously. With the advent of the personal digital assistant, continuous e-mail checking is becoming a fact of work life for more and more managers.

Time spent on e-mail has opportunity costs, of course. The pervasive use of e-mail has led to a decrease in face-to-face communications; we sometimes send e-mail to the person in the office next door rather than having a brief chat. As discussed in previous chapters, partnership development and staff communication demand time spent in meaningful dialogue to achieve a higher level of mutual understanding. The time we spend being "paced" by the electronic world has shifted the modes and often the quality of interaction.

E-mail also diminishes the quality of communication. E-mail removes layers of meaning that would be conveyed in person, through facial expression, tone, and body language for instance.[3] Because of the pace and volume, most of us read and write e-mail at top speed, instead of reading and writing slowly and carefully. The way we use e-mail often creates misunderstandings, mistakes, and communication gaps. The challenge is "to stop volume from simply overwhelming value."[3]

Electronic Fatigue Syndrome

Do any of these trends have a health impact? Several years ago, one of us was discussing these trends with another former NIOSH director, and we decided that a scientific article was needed on this subject. At that time, many articles were being written about the occurrence of a newly described condition—chronic fatigue syndrome. We decided to title the article "Electronic Fatigue Syndrome." Unfortunately, the prospective author was "too busy" responding to e-mail messages to write the article. Perhaps the term *killer app* has a double meaning.

If we apply basic principles of prevention (the cornerstone of public health) and of good management, certain practices emerge as ways to recognize and prevent the potential adverse effects of electronic fatigue syndrome. As a central principle, workers must take control of the technology, rather than letting the technology pace their workday. Recent research on the control of job stress has found that high job demands, lack of job control, and lack of special support are key predictors of the occurrence of stress-related adverse health outcomes.[4] Therefore, prevention of potential adverse effects of the overuse of e-mail should focus on ways to "limit exposure" and to develop concrete approaches by which individuals can control their interaction with the technology. One aspect of the prevention strategy is to develop better social systems to delineate "appropriate use" of e-mail.

Preventing Electronic Fatigue Syndrome

We suggest a few simple strategies:

1. Limit checking e-mail to specific time blocks: perhaps the start and end of each workday. By doing so, you will first condition yourself to control your own impulse to check e-mail more often than necessary, and you may be able to condition coworkers (especially those who report to you) to do the same. Most e-mail represents "urgent, not important" work.
2. Treat e-mail as we used to treat paper: handle each message only once. Respond, delete, or file. Avoid resending and avoid letting messages accumulate in your in-box.
3. Train software through the use of filters. For example, you can create filters to automatically file messages from specific Listservs into folders, or label as "junk" any message from a sender not in your address book.
4. Create a filing system, including an action file. Resist the urge to accumulate a mountain of e-mail messages in your files. Create a "five-week" file for messages that do not need to be saved forever, and then delete the messages once they are older than five weeks.

5. Use plain language. Think of the context in which people read your e-mail: be clear and concise:[5]

   - Short sentences, short paragraphs
   - Be clear and direct: focus on one issue
   - Use good document design (like signposts and headings)
   - Be aware of "referents" to prior e-mails that the recipient may not remember

6. Finally, do not manage by e-mail! Management is about relationships; e-mail is a way to share information. Although e-mail can help us be more efficient managers, it can get in the way and is not a substitute for the basic process of management and leadership discussed in this book.

Summary

Although e-mail can help us in our roles of managing and leading in an increasingly technology-driven work environment, we should be alert to the potential for electronic fatigue syndrome as more time and energy are directed into e-mail–related activity. We suggest that by limiting the time spent on e-mail very strictly, by developing techno-logic techniques to manage e-mail, and by avoiding the tendency to misuse e-mail, workers will enhance their control over this technology. Furthermore, by managers controlling the pace of work, rather than having pace controlled by e-mail, workplace stresses will be limited and managerial effectiveness will be maximized.

References

1. Hurrell JJ, Ariotequieter C. Occupational stress. In: Levy BS, Wegman DH, Baron SL, Sokas RK, eds. *Occupational and Environmental Health*. 5th ed. Philadelphia, PA: Lippincott Williams & Wilkins; 2006:382–396.

2. Overholt A. Intel's got (too much) mail. Available at: http://www.fastcompany.com/magazine/44/intel.html. Accessed March 1, 2006.

3. Brown JS, Duguid P. *The Social Life of Information*. Boston: Harvard Business School Press; 2002, xiii–2.

4. Karasak RA, Theorall T. *Healthy Work: Stress, Productivity, and the Reconstruction of Working Life*. New York: Basic Books; 1990.

5. Brenner R. 101 Tips for writing and managing email: a handbook for professionals. Available at: http://www. chacocanyon.com. 2005. Accessed March 1, 2006.

Chapter 20

Managing and New Web Communication Technology

Stephen N. Orton

In the previous chapter, we discussed how public health managers could control the pace of their work by controlling the technology they used for work, in particular, e-mail communications. In this chapter, we look at the larger world of Internet tools, taking a more optimistic view of their value to you as a public health manager. Even if you are a card-carrying Luddite, you will have heard that there is now a second generation of Web-based tools that go beyond sending an attachment via e-mail, searching a database, or buying a product from a worldwide inventory. This second-generation of tools is commonly referred to as "Web 2.0." Don't call it Web Twenty if you don't want savvy people to LOL: call it Web Two Point Oh. These tools are built to facilitate one-to-one and one-to-many communications. Under this heading fall a number of classes of Web-stuff like wikis, blogs, Web conferencing tools, video-share tools and podcasts, as well as brand-name communication tools such as Facebook, MySpace, Ning, WebEx, Adobe Connect, ooVoo, Del.ic.ious, Twitter, and probably several more that didn't exist last month.

There are much better ways for you to learn about these tools than to read about them in a book or a journal. Go online, watch a tutorial, find model sites, sit with a person who has recently attended college, try them out. Here, though, is a very brief classification of the different kinds of tools.

- Tools to store/deliver specific stuff (like video, audio, photos, links, documents)

135

- Tools to help you communicate in a group interested in one topic/project
- Tools to help one specific group communicate all in one place
- Tools to communicate out on a specific topic and hear back

In each category, you will find some tools designed to facilitate sharing in real time, or nearly real time—so that we're almost "talking" back and forth as we would on the phone. In fact, some tools are designed as supplements to phone conversations. Other tools are designed to facilitate sharing in situations when real time isn't possible or isn't important. And some tools blur that boundary.

Web 2.0: What Is It Good For?

What are the goals you might want to achieve that these tools could facilitate? They are many and varied. Let me suggest a few possibilities based on my own experience and knowledge, but understand that this is not an exhaustive list. Internally, these tools might help work groups share more effectively and manage their work processes better. These tools might store knowledge better, so that new people joining an effort can track what's happened or so that managers can see what's happening across a broad effort. A social networking tool or a wiki could store documents and threaded discussions on a specific project, for instance. These tools might open up channels for more people to provide input in the design phase of a project. A webinar could help designers share draft materials broadly and get feedback (audio, text, or responses to poll questions). They might permit workgroups that are separated geographically to work closely on a specific work product: GoogleDocs, for example, allows individuals to simultaneously open and edit a single text document or spreadsheet even if they are thousands of miles apart. A video channel added to a phone meeting (e.g., ooVoo) might allow the group to stay engaged longer and pick up more easily on nonverbal cues that help the group get the right answer more quickly. The tools might simplify your reporting at the end of a work process by allowing you to track inputs over time by reviewing date stamps.

Externally, the tools might allow you to engage distant/busy partners who otherwise couldn't attend a sit-down meeting. They might allow useful, anonymous comments on an important question; a manager I know uses the poll feature on her webinars to allow all stakeholders to quickly and painlessly give proposals a thumbs-up or thumbs-down, without fear of embarrassment or retribution. The tools might allow you to share material in formats other than text—video or audio, for example—and thus improve your ability to influence key stakeholders. They might allow you to have influence over a decision or a process even though you are separated from the traditional power sources.

The challenge of whether or how to use these tools really is much more a management challenge than a technical challenge. These Web 2.0 tools are vessels for storing/delivering information, especially kinds of information that the first generation of Internet tools (static Web pages and e-mail) aren't especially well equipped to handle. The different "specialty" vessels have specific jobs they are equipped to do well. Many of the technological issues are solved (or solvable) at this point: engineers and developers have done the foundational work and are busily making the tools simpler and fussing around the edges to serve specific niches. More difficult by far—for you as a manager—is the challenge of getting actual people to use the tools to do actual work, and like it.

Case in Point

Communication starts with people. Take this chapter for instance. In writing this chapter, we imagine a set of readers who are forward thinking managers in organizations concerned with population health. You are the top 20% kind of people, continuing to learn new things, trying out new ways of doing things, looking for ways to sharpen your existing tools and maybe try out some new ones. You are the kind of people, in short, who are wondering how to integrate new Web 2.0 communication tools into your work as managers—if you haven't already. Given the demographics of governmental public health in particular, many of you have been out of school and in the work world for 20 or 30 years. That's not true of the whole group, however. Some are more recently out of school; maybe you've been lucky enough to find a meaningful career track in public health and are eager to keep learning and figure out how to get the most out of your skills and knowledge. Although many in our audience work in the government and academic sectors, some work for nonprofits, some for healthcare organizations, some for foundations, a few in the corporate sector.

In other words, the group is not especially homogenous. We have a wide range of academic and experiential backgrounds. We share interests in public health and management, but our backgrounds and assumptions and even our set of acronyms can be very different. Our diversity has many benefits, certainly. Ideally, it improves our ability to get the right answer in a team situation; we won't have an echo-chamber effect where everyone already thinks the same way. We are able to attack complex problems from multiple angles. In terms of communication, though, diversity is also a potential barrier.

Our ability to communicate is additionally hampered by structure and geography. Public health is a very decentralized system. It has been called a cottage industry: there are a few federal and state-level systems for directly protecting health, but the lion's share of the work gets done at the community level. Historically, it has been a struggle to open communication across communities; across the barriers between local, state, national, and federal systems; across the barriers between program areas; across the barriers between government and nonprofit sectors.

This book represents one effort to communicate across all these barriers, geographic, organizational, generational, and academic. The mechanism is ink on paper. The discourse is all one-way, from editorialist out. Because this is the 21st century, computers and the Internet have played a critical role in your ability to find and read these words. They are being composed on a screen but stored and shared digitally on an intranet; they will be sent to an editor via e-mail; they will appear in a book that will be marketed on the Internet. You might have discovered the existence of this chapter using a web library search tool, or found the book on Amazon.com.

Note that all of these functions of the Internet are 10 years old, at least. Some people say that government is 20 years behind the private sector—but in the Internet world, months are like years. On the Internet, the government should be only a year and a half behind the private sector!

The promise of Web 2.0 technology is to speed up and broaden out the sharing process. This chapter is going to take months to reach you. Your experience in reading it will likely be solitary. You will have the option of looking up the e-mail address or phone number of the author if you are moved to reply—but you almost certainly won't bother. Much more difficult will be for you to find the other people who are reading the chapter and also finding it interesting—or finding it flawed in some way and wanting to add some material to it! As a reader, those are the people you might really want to hear from: the other readers who were seeking the same information you were, and who may very well have a piece of information you want.

This is the problem that Web 2.0 tools mean to address: these tools allow the barriers between writers and readers to break down. Readers can become writers, adding their voices and perspectives in response to what the written work says, such that monologue could become dialogue. And that dialogue will be (more or less) permanent, so that readers coming along later can read it. To demonstrate how this might feel, let me give you an example from a nontechnology setting. I attended a session at a national meeting several years ago. It started out poorly—the presenter had presented on the topic many times before, and she was jumping from one slide to another in a huge deck of hundreds of PowerPoint slides she had compiled on the topic. She lost her place, and while she searched for a specific slide, a discussion broke out: one listener asked a question, and another listener proposed a framework, and two more jumped in with examples and perspectives. The presenter got drawn into the conversation. After 20 minutes, the group had proposed and discussed a whole set of questions that were of interest to the group in the room (questions only tangentially related to what the speaker had originally intended to say). It is to this day one of the most memorable conference sessions I've ever attended. A good blog, or wiki, or social networking site, is trying to help make this kind of result happen on purpose.

Promise and Pitfalls

This analysis suggests the promise, and the pitfalls, in new communication technology. The promise is clear:

- Break down physical barriers (like geography and time), expand access
- Maximize the potential for diverse groups to create and share knowledge
- Facilitate return communication, get past "one-way" broadcast mode

The pitfalls will be equally clear. First, these tools will require people and organizations to change, and many will resist that change. Managing the change process will be tricky in the best of circumstances. The tools can help barriers get broken—but they don't actually break the barriers themselves. You have to do that. Choosing the wrong technology for the job will create a backlash worse than any communication problem you have currently: if you and your stakeholders hack away at the old barriers with the wrong tool, soon you will be sweaty and frustrated.

Second, the promise of breaking down barriers comes at a price. These tools, naturally, substitute a new set of barriers for the old ones. Understand these new barriers. The "digital divide" is real and might put key stakeholders out of reach, depending on the communities you serve. Government agencies in particular may have security issues with some Web 2.0 technologies. Some users have a hard time engaging with Internet-mediated discussions; these discussions can feel "cold" in the absence of social cues that help us understand each other when we meet in person. Overuse can become a barrier to achieving your goals as well. The same human tendency that results in the overuse of e-mail will inevitably drive some to overuse Web 2.0 technologies: you may want to start a new wiki for every project, even when a wiki isn't really appropriate for the job. In some cases, the technology will somehow become the main point and people will lose sight of the original goal entirely.

The third pitfall is a sort of boomerang: the cost of not trying the new technology may be more than you can afford. Trying Web 2.0 shows partners and staff that the organization is on the cutting edge. Not trying shows the reverse. Good managers scan the environment for change; you are trying to achieve organizational goals, so you watch out for barriers and look for new ways to get where you want to go more quickly. Web 2.0 is a set of tools for doing the work, but in one sense, it is also an environmental change to be aware of in itself—a leading edge of the ongoing change represented by the Internet. We can all agree that the Internet has created changes in the environment for public health organizations. We work differently now. We recruit workers differently; we disseminate information differently, collect and use data differently, interact with our customers differently. The new Web 2.0 tools represent a specific new part of that environmental change. Many of the people we want to manage—partners, customers, and workers in our own organizations—are already using these new tools. Other people we want to manage—including perhaps the traditional-but-forward-thinking boss—are not using the tools but want the organization to learn them and use them. Many of us are accountable to people who want to know "what are we doing with Web 2.0?"

The following tips might help you avoid the pitfalls involved with managing with Web 2.0 technology:

1. PICK THE RIGHT TOOL.

Understand what the tool can and can't do, and if you are pushing a specific tool, don't overpromise. More important, attend to the specific needs of the people/group you hope will use the tool. What does the group need to share? Why do they need to share it? What are the real-world goals to be met? What you are attempting here is behavior change. You are trying to get people to work differently, in order to achieve some higher-order benefit. You want a change far beyond somebody thinking "yep, technology sure is amazing" (and you'd like to rule out "yep, technology sure does suck").

2. FOCUS ON OUTCOMES.

Be up-front with the group about what you hope to accomplish by using the new technology. Come up with measures that will show whether the effort to switch has been worth it—because it will take some effort. For a while, a group might be willing to learn a new tool for the sake of newness, but before long the group will want to confirm that the new tool works better than the old tool for accomplishing a job.

3. ATTEND TO THE PEOPLE.

Teams in our hard-driving culture often founder on the rocks of process. We tend to dive into task mode, skipping over the discussion of roles, responsibilities, how to work together best. As a result, we lose traction and team energy dissipates. Sometimes team members drift away, unsure how to help or how to be heard, or unconvinced that it makes any difference. In many cases, Web 2.0 will represent a new process. Talk about how that new process is working for the people on the team. Who is being heard? How are leadership and power being expressed? How is the team compensating for the lack of human contact and social cues that would typically keep them connected and supported emotionally?

4. DON'T EXPECT HARD PROBLEMS TO HAVE EASY SOLUTIONS.

Don't convince yourself—and certainly don't tell your stakeholders—that you have a "simple" technological solution to a problem that so far has been intractable. Why is a particular stakeholder group unwilling to move forward? Maybe it is because they are geographically distant and have trouble meeting face to face. Maybe, though, it is because the issue on the table is a difficult issue. An Internet "solution" might exacerbate the group's inertia, increase the chances of hurt feelings, or accidentally marginalize some stakeholders.

5. TAKE A RISK; DARE TO FAIL.
Innovation is highly dependent on the willingness to fail. You have to learn what doesn't work. Where, under what circumstances, are you willing to fail—in exchange for the promise of better results in the future? Set up "laboratories" for yourself. Start trying new technologies and new processes, on purpose, acknowledging to the group that you are trying to "fail forward faster" to a better way of working. Maybe you will have to make small bets at first. Just start. Understand that you will get credit for trying in any case. And understand that you will get additional credit for failing, as long as you learn something in the process that increases the chances for success the next time around.

Putting Web Tools to Work

My goal here is not to tell you which of these Web tools to use (depends on your context), or how to use them (what's the Web for if not that?). I am not going to tell you that these tools are essential and that ignoring them will sabotage your career. I can neither aver that these tools are "flavor-of-the-month" fads that will be gone in a year, nor tell you which ones will have the staying power of the telephone and e-mail. I can tell you this: while we'll always need telephones, e-mail is now considered by some an outmoded form of communication for work. A colleague of mine says that we have overused it: we have tried to make it perform a whole range of functions for which it is not designed.

The more general point I want to make is that when you use these tools as a manager, understand that they are tools. They are not "solutions," and they are not toys. This advice has different implications, depending on your side of the digital divide. If you are an early adapter and already know the tools inside and out, don't convince yourself that these tools will solve all your communication problems: learn what the tool can really do for people. On the other side of the digital divide, where the tools themselves are still confusing to you, don't think that you can fake it based on a cursory understanding of the tool: learn what the tool can really do for people. The question for both groups is this: what is the human problem to which this tool is a solution?

Either way, there is plenty of time to get Web 2.0 right. If you are on the bleeding edge, slow down and bring your group along with you. Be satisfied with small steps to start with. Take the time to really get it right; listen to the people in your group who are struggling with the rationale and the objectives; make sure you really are improving the process and getting the results you intend. If you feel you are being left in the dust by technological change, start learning one tool. It's OK that you aren't using them all yet. Accept the humble but noble position of learner; be willing to look silly for a little while as you practice. Recognize that the race goes not always to the swift.

Chapter 21

Managing the Difficult Conversation

Claudia S. Plaisted Fernandez

Managers are often faced with the dreaded "difficult conversation." For some people, this event is so terrifying that they employ the ostrich strategy, avoiding the event altogether and living in denial of the serious problems their organizations face. Good managers practice the art of the difficult conversation. This requires patience, calmness, and objectivity—what author Ronald Heifetz might call "getting on the balcony."[1,2] But the artist of the difficult conversation understands that getting on the balcony is not enough—you need to get others there too.

When people are caught in a contentious issue, they come to the table with their position staked out in the sand: "my team needs that office space!", "our budget allocation must be . . . ," "my line of authority includes . . .". Whatever the issue: territory, power, symbols, money, resources, time—they come with a goal and an I *want* position.

Lucky for managers, there are some simple tools to take the terror out of holding difficult conversations. The first tool is a classic: whole-heart listening. You might have heard this described as active listening.[3,4] Whole-heart listening is when your total attention is devoted to hearing what the other person is saying and not to enumerating the flaws in their argument or planning what you are going to say in response. Whole-heart listening, without judgment, helps people feel heard.

Chapter Source: © 2008 Wolters Kluwer Health | Lippincott Williams & Wilkins. Originally published in *J Public Health Management Practice.* 2008; 14(3): 317–319.

145

Another tool for facilitating difficult conversations is letting the person know what you heard them say. Rephrase their concerns using different words. Do not merely parrot the words they said: rephrasing helps you both gain clarity. Then, reflect the emotional content of what they are saying. To feel heard, people sometimes need an acknowledgment of their frustration, anxiety, anger, or sense of injustice about the situation. The kinds of statements you might find helpful to move the dialogue along include the following:

> I can imagine that you must be feeling some anxiety over this.
> I hear the tension in your voice; please tell me more about your concerns.
> You sound very frustrated with this situation.

You might even consider saying something like, "I'm feeling a bit anxious about this conversation. It seems that we're talking mostly about blame and not about the deeper issues." Recognizing and sharing your own feelings can help you manage the emotional side of a difficult conversation.

You cannot just avoid this emotional side altogether. If you are going to excel at the art of the difficult conversation, you have to realize that humans are emotional beings. Some are more in touch with their emotional sides, and some are more sharing about them, but essentially we are all creatures of feeling. When it comes to difficult conversations, it is very likely that at least one party to the exchange will be feeling some sense of crisis. People in crisis are more likely to be influenced by their feelings, beliefs, perspectives, and needs than they are when the stakes are not so high. Not acknowledging these feelings, beliefs, and perspectives will not make them go away.

Difficult solutions require what Ron Heifetz, in *Leadership without Easy Answers*, terms *adaptive work*. Essentially, adaptive work means personal change. To practice the art of the difficult conversation, you have to be able to lead others through the required change: the change of perspectives, beliefs, needs, and feelings. One way to accomplish this change is through reframing. Reframing puts the issue in a different context. Someone could complain to you: "Listening to their whining is a waste of my valuable time." You can acknowledge their frustration but reframe the issue so that they see the importance of "listening to whining"—that, in fact, listening to complaints may be the most important part of what they do every day. You have reframed the issue such that they now see value in something and a renewed sense of commitment to it.

The paramount tool for managing difficult conversations is to help people move from a focus on their "positions" to an understanding of their "interests." If you draw a picture of where two people of opposing desires stand on an issue, you could place two dots far apart and draw a line between them. Those are two opposing points—their positions. But if you draw large circles around these points, you depict the field of their interests. You can get people to think about their interests by helping them talk about what they want to accomplish through their desired action. For example, two colleagues may have opposite ideas about how to address a problem—but both have the same *interest* in solving the same problem: there is common ground.

Thinking in terms of positions versus interests creates a conversation that encompasses a range of concerns. Get your parties talking enough and you will very likely find that there are areas where their circles of interest overlap. Still having trouble? Push back the parameters to widen the sphere of consideration. For example, if you cannot agree on a course of action to take over the next five years, can you agree on where it should go in 50? That is the circle of widest agreement technique. The people in these discussions will not be in their current jobs in 50 years. The stakes are lower, and it is much easier to achieve agreement. One area of agreement makes others easier to arrive at. For more on this technique, I suggest reading *Getting to Yes*, an excellent guide to negotiation strategy by Fisher and Ury.[5]

Here is another example: a disgruntled employee—say, it is a man who has been with your organization for years—is talking ill about the department or team. Rumor gets back to you of this bad advertising. Do you reprimand the individual? Order him to cease expressing his opinion? Fire him? Do nothing? All those strategies come from the "company position" that unacceptable speech should be stopped. But what is your *interest*? Reprimanding, squelching, firing, or ignoring is not likely to stop the bad-talking. They are more likely to spread it around and make it look justified. Assuming this person is a productive and valuable employee, what might be his interest in talking this way? Is he struggling with an organizational change or something similar? Is he disgruntled, feeling unappreciated, powerless, or voiceless? Maybe someone else was chosen for a promotion or attractive job assignment. If so, his *interest* is to become less disgruntled, feel more appreciated, have more power, or be heard. His goal is not to trash the organization but to become an engaged employee once again. In fact, as his manager, that is your goal, too!

You need to understand that people do not express this kind of dissatisfaction because they got out of bed on the wrong side or because of some personal deficiency. Usually, it is based on their perceptions—their truth—of the organization. If their truth is *the* truth, then you as a manager have a task ahead of you far more challenging than successfully managing a difficult conversation—you have the task of examining and amending your organizational culture. However, let us assume that their view, their position, is slightly skewed from reality. Then, the good manager invests in them to help them gain insight into what they are feeling and why (listening, reflecting, reframing)—and helps them find the path to a more satisfying perspective of the organization. It is hoped this is a more rational truth of the organization.

Table 21-1
Artful Tools for Moving from Positions to Interests
Identifying feelings around the issue
Describe position in detail (to uncover interests)
Describe the other person's position/perspective
Have each person argue for the other person's point (to help each party gain perspective)
Reframe the position statements to reflect underlying interests
Gain agreement on the widest circle of interests (far in the future, at the highest level or most fundamental level)

Source: © 2008 Wolters Kluwer Health | Lippincott Williams & Wilkins. Originally published in J Public Health Management Practice. 2008; 14(3): 317–319.

Table 21-2
Guidelines to Follow for Managing Difficult Conversation
Steps to avoid
Threaten
Accuse
Give orders to start or cease a behavior/action
Give into the demands of the other party
Be judgmental
Defend and justify the action/decision under dispute
Become defensive
Steps to take
Inquire about the feelings of the other party and help him/her understand those feelings
Gain agreement on the overall interests of the group or the team
Help each party put him or herself in the shoes of the other
Help the parties see the larger picture of the situation
Affirm the role and value of each party to the group
Provide hope for engagement in valued work in the future

Source: © 2008 Wolters Kluwer Health | Lippincott Williams & Wilkins. Originally published in J Public Health Management Practice. 2008; 14(3): 317–319.

In this case, the goal is to help the employee see that he has a vested interest in the achievements, success, and reputation of the team or department and that success will bring new opportunities for interesting and rewarding work.

Once you gain comfort with these simple tools, you will be amazed at how much easier managing the difficult conversation becomes (see Tables 21-1 and 21-2).

References

1. Heifetz RA. *Leadership without Easy Answers.* Cambridge, MA: Harvard University Press; 1994.
2. Heifetz RA, Linsky M. *Leadership on the Line: Staying Alive through the Dangers of Leading.* Boston, MA: Harvard Business School Press; 2002.
3. Landsberger J. Study guides and strategies: active listening. Available at: http://www.studygs.net/listening.htm. Accessed March 7, 2008.
4. Conflict Research Consortium, Online Training Program on Intractable Conflict (OTPIC). Conflict management and constructive confrontation: a guide to the theory and practice. Available at: http://www.colorado.edu/conflict/peace/treatment/activel.htm. Accessed March 7, 2008.
5. Fisher R, Ury W. *Getting to Yes: Negotiating Agreement without Giving In.* New York: Penguin Books; 1991.

Chapter 22

Managing the Boss

Janet E. Porter and Edward L. Baker, Jr.

Years ago, a colleague, Brian, spent months bitterly complaining about his boss and how hard she was to work for. In an effort to help Brian sort out what type of person he worked well with, Brian was asked how many bosses he had had during his career. After reflecting for a minute, Brian replied, "Five." Asked which of the five bosses he had really liked, Brian reflected even longer before answering, "None of them." That revelation meant that the problem was not—as previously thought—the impossible boss but instead that Brian did not like working for anybody, and probably should be his own boss. Shortly thereafter, Brian left that job and went into business for himself because he understood that he thrived on working independently.

Most of us aren't going into business for ourselves, as Brian did. Rather, if you work in public health, it is more than likely that you have a boss, a supervisor, a board: someone to whom you are accountable. You may be lucky and only have one boss, but even under that scenario, you still have other stakeholders who you have to please to get your work done and to keep your job.

We know from Gallup poll research, reported in *First, Break All the Rules*,[1] that the old adage: "Employees don't leave their job, they leave their bosses" is true. And, oftentimes, we think about that truism and reflect on how wonderful the world of employment would be if managers were

Chapter Source: © 2005 Wolters Kluwer Health | Lippincott Williams & Wilkins. Originally published in *J Public Health Management Practice*. 2005; 11(1): 90–93.

simply easier to work for. But let's turn that around and think about what public health staff and managers can do to have better relationships with their bosses. Within organizational structures, a key to success and promotion is your relationship with your boss. We tend to think about managing those who report to us rather than managing those we report to. But what are the tips to successful boss management?

Tip 1: Know Yourself and Pick a Boss Who Fits With You

The first key to success is to diligently interview the person you'll be working for at the same time they are interviewing you to determine whether there is a good fit. In job interviewing situations where you are anxious to make a good impression, it is challenging to be equally discerning to determine whether this person is someone you want to work for. You are trying to figure out whether you are compatible; the key to insight about compatibility is knowing what is important to you in a prospective boss. As Jeff, a public health official, stated, "I've decided that the most important characteristics for me in a boss are someone who is smart, works hard, and can be trusted. At this point in my career, I only want to work for people I respect, and I don't respect people who aren't smart, hard-working, or trustworthy." You cannot screen out "bad boss fits" with your work style unless you can be as succinct as Jeff. Do you know what is essential to you in selecting the ideal boss? One trick for determining the ideal boss is to take index cards and write one of the following words on each card: participatory, decisive, smart, trustworthy, loyal, resourceful, connected, strategic, honest, team-builder, coach, empowering, patient, dependable, organized, respected, and secure; then put the cards in order. Do you, at this stage of your career, most want to work for someone who is a good coach or someone who is connected? Those are the choices you will have to make about the relative importance of various characteristics.

The best people to tell you what your potential new boss is like are his or her current direct reports. Meeting individually with them and asking them pointed questions about what the person is like to work for is essential—but can be politically tricky. So, simply ask direct reports to relate a story about the boss that illustrates the person's work style and values. Then, listen carefully to the stories you hear and think about what picture they paint.

Look for the longevity on the team as you interview. If everyone is new, that tells you something. High turnover of staff should be a major warning sign and worthy of scrutiny. If they are all lifers, that tells you something too. If you want a boss who will nurture your career and provide you opportunities for growth, you need to listen for stories of people who have gone on to positions of greater responsibility after being groomed by your new boss.

Naturally, as you meet the team, you will be trying to evaluate whether these are individuals you want to work with. Do they seem passionate and competent and fun? But beyond seeing them as potential colleagues, reflect for a moment on what the team says about what the boss values. For example, if the boss selects and promotes individuals who are highly competent but averse to change and primarily promote the status quo, then you have to determine whether this is an organization that will stimulate your personal need for change and challenge.

What we want in the person we work for evolves over time. Patience is key when you are young in your career. It is natural to want to work for someone who has scheduled an organized orientation to your new job and patiently teaches you all the policies and procedures. You want someone who is there for you, answering your questions, and pointing you in the right direction. But then over time, managers evolve to wanting to work for someone who leaves them alone, someone who trusts them and empowers them to do their job. When selecting a new opportunity, evaluate all the dimensions of the job—with special emphasis on your perceived compatibility with your new boss.

Tip 2: Have Your Boss Define Success for You

How many times have you heard someone despair, "I just don't know what my boss wants!" Well, the best way to find out is to ask. The core question is, "If I am really successful in my job, a year from now, what will have happened?" In other words, "What constitutes a home run?" It is amazing the number of people who cannot answer that question about someone they've reported to for many years.

Sandy, a manager who had been in her job for 15 years, was lamenting that she was being replaced. She offered, "There has never been a major mistake in my entire time here. How can they do this to me?" When it was pointed out that perhaps the employer wanted change, wanted the organization to be dynamic and responsive to the community, and that risk-free program management might not be what the organization valued, Sandy commented, "But that is ridiculous! Who would want to hire a manager who made mistakes!" Sandy could literally not see that she worked for someone who tolerated mistakes, as long as there was innovation and learning from those mistakes. Sadly, Sandy had never asked her boss—who was the same individual during that entire 15 years—to define success. Perhaps more important, Sandy had not observed the behavior of her peers and tried to determine what characteristics of those peers made them so successful. Rather, Sandy chose to attribute their success to personal favoritism— rather than seeing that their behavior reflected what the boss valued: the creation of a dynamic, enterprising organization highly responsive to the communities they served.

Ideally, you want a boss who can say what she or he wants the outcome of the work to be and can provide guidance on concerns or suggestions that relate to achieving the outcome. Further, it is best that the boss not say too much about how you achieve the outcome; you should be given the responsibility to figure that out.

Tip 3: Agree on Communication Style

Because management is all about communication, it is critical that you have a meeting of the minds with your boss about how often you will communicate, how much detail you will provide, what types of problems or challenges she wants to be involved with, and how formal or informal she wants to be. Agreeing on the frequency of individual or team meetings is the first step. But after reaching agreement on that, the next question is, What does the boss want to know? For example, at the North Carolina Institute for Public Health, we take great pride in our partnerships. Thus, those in management are really interested in knowing when partnerships are not going well. When agreements with other public health organizations or schools on campus are being negotiated that establish the framework for the working relationship, management wants to know. But lots of other decisions related to program design or cost or location are totally within the purview of staff. So, knowing what the organization values and what types of information need to be transmitted to stakeholders is key.

Central to good communication is understanding the depth of detail expected. One public health manager could not restrain herself from explaining how the clock got built whenever she was asked what time it was. Despite repeated coaching that her boss valued brevity of communication above everything else, she persisted in giving him far more information than he wanted—to the detriment of their working relationship. Clearly, communication style is a broader indication of overall management style. The boss who empowers probably wants less information, whereas the boss who wants details may tend to micromanage.

Knowing how your boss wants to be told is equally key. Some managers are averse to e-mail (and particularly hearing bad news via e-mail) and want to be told personally or by voicemail at the very least. So, reaching agreement and asking the right questions, about what and how and when the boss wants to receive information and be involved in decision making is central to having a good relationship.

An operating principle for most managers is "no surprises." While that is a good credo, the next question is, What doesn't she want to be surprised about? So understanding what constitutes a big issue relative to financial performance, community relations, staffing problems, or public relations issues is essential to staying out of trouble. Ask your boss about the "no surprises" rule. Some feel more strongly than others about this.

Tip 4: Be Flexible

Janey, a public health manager with a record of success, could never warm up to her new boss, who was seen as highly effective but aloof. While others commented on how much they enjoyed working with the new boss, Janey was at a loss as to how to develop the close personal relationship—even friendship—that she had with her previous supervisors. She was disappointed that despite repeated attempts to socialize with her boss, she still did not know her the way she wanted to. Because Janey had a high need for affiliation, she needed to be personally connected to her boss. Her inability to adapt to a more reserved style left her feeling so disconnected that she finally took another job.

While it is important to know yourself (see Tip #1), it is also important to be flexible and to allow your boss to define the format of the relationship. If you are in touch with your core values and appreciate that those core values are being met, then you can let go of areas where the boss falls short of meeting your desired relationship. For example, if you thrived on the opportunities for community involvement stimulated by your boss in your previous job but those opportunities are not available now, perhaps you can find an outlet for getting involved in the community in a meaningful way outside your job. The question is whether that dimension of your relationship with your boss is essential or merely desired. In short, it is your job to adapt to your boss's style, not vice versa.

Tip 5: Understand Whose Opinion the Boss Values

Fred commented that the most valuable lesson he learned in his public health internship was to get along with the boss's secretary. That was a hard-fought lesson since his first boss's secretary decided she didn't like Fred and sabotaged every project he worked on during his internship. Whether it is the secretary or the board of health or the next-door neighbor, knowing whose opinion your boss values and from whom he or she will get information about your performance should shape who you work to develop relationships with. For many years, one of the most popular elective courses at Harvard's MBA program was Organizational Politics. When a graduate was asked what she got out of the course, she commented, "If you want to influence the organization, influence your boss; if you want to influence your boss, find out who influences him or her." That says it all.

Upward Mobility

These five tips relate not only to the success in your current job but also in positioning yourself for opportunities. Career opportunities come about because people in positions of power and influence think highly enough of some staff that they promote their talents and potential to others. If you want to maximize the opportunities available to you in your career, stop and evaluate how your relationship is with your boss on a regular basis and be objective about the role you are playing in enhancing or hurting that relationship.

In summary, we suggest that you give special attention to managing the relationship with your boss, both in the process of deciding whether to accept a new position or within the daily interaction with your current boss. We often say that "relationships are primary, everything else is derivative." In no other work relationship is this more true, than with your boss.

For more information about the North Carolina Institute for Public Health, go to: http://www.sph.unc.edu/nciph.

Reference

1.   Buckingham M, Coffman, C. *First, Break All the Rules*. New York, NY: Simon & Schuster; 1999.

Section **IV**

Managing
Business

Civic Entrepreneurship: Revenue-Generating Strategies for Government and Nonprofit Organizations

James H. Johnson, Jr.

Public health managers are expected to have expertise across a broad spectrum of public health competences, but to actually *do* anything about the challenges that face their communities, they need to be able to obtain resources. In the past, this may have been simply a matter of waiting for the federal, state, or local monies to come in or writing a grant application for foundational funding. But times are changing. As federal resources are getting scarcer, federal mandates seem to be getting more burdensome. Private foundations want more accountability from their grantees as well. Granting organizations are now using the word "sustainable" to mean that they will not fund anything indefinitely: they want you to design a program that will eventually (in as little as a couple years) fund itself. What that means in the real world is that by the time you figure out what to do and how to do it, you are out of grant money. If your program is not sustainable on its own, don't even think of having time to evaluate whether it works.

The changes are not all negative. For many reasons, there has been a rise in recent years in venture philanthropy and social entrepreneurship. Entrepreneurial leaders see in the current fiscal crisis an opportunity to reach public health goals without becoming caught in the "unfunded-mandate" trap or the "perpetual-grant-seeking" trap. This is the opportunity: the opportunity to take control of your own agenda. Entrepreneurial public health leaders will have their organizations solving problems rather than responding to requests for proposals and

159

writing reports. Your communities should be able to depend upon services being there beyond the funding cycle. Your local companies want to invest in their communities and reap the rewards of having a healthy workforce and creating positive community relations.

In this chapter, I will describe strategies for becoming a "civic entrepreneur"—making sound business decisions that allow public sector leaders to be creators, rather than mere redistributors, of wealth.

Civic Entrepreneurship

To be a civic entrepreneur requires both a mind-set and a set of skills. The mind-set is, as stated above, to stop thinking only in terms of the social welfare orientation toward public health work and begin thinking of yourself as an entrepreneur: one who uses the efficiency and innovation often associated with good business leaders to get resources for creating and sustaining great public health programs. The goal of this mind-set is to create social value where there was only need and dependency.

The skill set of the civic entrepreneur includes the following:

- Ability to assess and clearly articulate the mission of the organization and the needs of the community served.
- Accountability to the constituencies served, including fiscal responsibility: be efficient with resources and create valuable outcomes for users and payers.
- Creativity and relentlessness in pursuing new opportunities to serve that mission.

Now, what can you do to put this mind-set and these skills into action? The following examples are meant to inspire you to find your own way to financial independence. They all have potential pitfalls, which we'll get to, but first let's consider the opportunities.

Revenue Generation Options and Examples

The key to civic entrepreneurial action is to forge strategic alliances across the spectrum of nonprofit, governmental, and for-profit arenas, with the goal of obtaining resources for programs and activities that further your mission. A strategic alliance is a win-win relationship that serves the needs of both organizations as it serves community needs. These can be pretty simple agreements, such as cause-related marketing alliances, in which a corporation donates a specified amount of cash, food, or equipment in direct proportion to sales revenue to support a specific cause. Such initiatives enhance the company's bottom line, while contributing to the resolution of pressing societal problems. You may have an American Express card linked to the Charge Against Hunger campaign, for example, or, rather than selling cookies, wrapping paper, or dish towel calendars, your child's school may have asked you to go to SchoolPop.com to support the school when you do your online shopping. Public health examples include Avon's "Kiss Goodbye to Breast Cancer" campaign, or American Express' "Charge for the Cure," both of which benefit the Komen Foundation. These are national examples, but you can think locally about the same kinds of alliances. Consider partnering with a sporting goods store or a workout facility. They get to tout their connection with a trusted public entity and perhaps increase their market share, and you could get funding for programs that encourage physical activity and ultimately a lever to improve population health.

Selling space is simple: companies get the use of a space and the space's owners get paid for the privilege. Spaces that might be relevant to a government or nonprofit entity include billboards, telephone kiosks, trash cans, buses, ATMs, computer screen savers, cafeteria menus, book covers, school rooftops, fruit, scoreboards, and fences. Consider partnering with a hospital that might pay for a mobile van to be used by the public health department in exchange for being able to advertise on the van. Or, give your clients cloth grocery bags with logos from a local store to encourage them to buy healthy food and save on plastic bag waste. You could print healthy diet suggestions on the other side of the bag.

In a final example, some nonprofits launch their own commercial or nonprofit ventures to support their work. The following are examples of the forms these ventures can take, and nonprofits that have tried them:

Products: Habitat for Humanity—T-shirts, gifts

Services: Nature Conservancy—educational tours

Storefronts: The World Wildlife Fund Canada

Online shops: American Civil Liberties Union

Many governmental public health agencies have found ways to spin off nonprofits that help support population health. Public health related ideas include selling T-shirts with the public health logo on the front and immunization schedule on the back to support childhood immunization programs; selling services you now offer for free: training on safe food handling for local restaurants, on-site preventive screenings for local industries' employees, prison health services; publishing a "healthy diet" cookbook.

These are just a few examples of revenue-generating possibilities. Others include exclusive agreements, such as pouring rights for a bottled water company, with profits going to exercise programs. Or, affinity programs, such as cobranded credit cards. You could form an alliance with local farmers and create "food credit cards" for use at their booths at the farmers' market. It's not a leap to imagine a group of health departments getting together to "brand" their organizations and partner with local or even more nationally based corporations to get a share in profits. Incentive programs, such as the familiar General Mills Box Tops for Education program, could work on a smaller scale: how about plastic bags for immunization? The possibilities are out there. Most of the ideas listed here have at least been tried. Many have already been executed. And some have failed (or haven't succeeded . . . yet). First, though, you have to try.

Benefits of Strategic Alliances

Both partners benefit from all of these types of strategic alliances. Benefits to the nonprofit/government entity include increased revenue; access to resources beyond money, including, for example, space, expertise, and a customer base; and, of course, an enhanced ability to offer services without worrying about the funding cycle. Corporations are able through such alliances to build customer loyalty by linking their name with a trusted public entity and cause, enhance public relations, and gain access to new markets. In the case of public health alliances, there is the added benefit to the corporation that the public, which includes their workforce, may end up healthier, a not-insignificant consideration in this era of skyrocketing healthcare costs.

An exercise we give to public health managers first learning about civic entrepreneurship is to brainstorm the craziest, most off-the-wall ideas for forging strategic alliances and generating revenue. We encourage them to think locally: in general, local public health should look locally for partners because it is the local businesses that will have a stake in the local public health organization's success. After brainstorming, we do with these ideas what usually gets done with crazy ideas: we wad them up and throw them away. The lesson is this: don't quit on your ideas. Some of them are crazy, but some are crazy-smart.

Some of them just might work, with consideration of a few crucial steps to take and pitfalls to watch out for.

Steps to Creating a Strategic Alliance or Commercial Business Venture

Keep several things in mind when preparing to forge a strategic alliance or commercial business venture. First, target a company you might like to work with and research the company's history of donations and future plans for charitable contributions. Work to understand their motivations, so that when you approach them you can present your added value—what you bring to the table—in terms that they understand and respect. Recognize that businesses don't like partnerships. A "strategic alliance" is an agreement to work together on one specific thing, with a clear set of objectives and goals. "Partnership" by contrast suggests a broad, amorphous commitment without any clear goal or end. Ally yourself with organizations whose skills and expertise complement and mesh with yours, not ones with exactly the same skills, or ones whose skills or expertise will not take you where you want to go.

Speaking of where you want to go, the most important thing to remember is to begin with the end in mind: know, at the outset, what exact outcomes you want to achieve, and state them clearly. If you know and can articulate the goals, it will be easier to do another important step, which is to get buy-in internally and externally. With a strategic group created expressly for this purpose, proceed by brainstorming ideas, conducting feasibility studies and, finally, developing a business plan. You will need a detailed, written, financially sound plan to get where you need to go. This last step is covered in the next chapter.

Potential Pitfalls

The first question you must answer in considering these types of strategic alliances is, "What will our stakeholders think?" Any or all of your stakeholders—for instance, the public, local or state politicians, taxpayers, other funders—might perceive any form of revenue generation as a move away from the public institution's mission. Spend time vetting your potential partners to make sure there is not a real conflict of interest.

At the same time, educate your stakeholders. They will need to know your mission and what it really costs to accomplish the goals that have been set for your organization. Generating revenue does not mean making a profit. Like everyone else, public institutions must find a way to pay for what they do in order to continue doing it. No money, no mission.

The second potential pitfall is a practical consideration: there will be limitations on what is available to launch your venture. A lot of work has to be done before any revenue is generated. This is where obtaining buy-in both internally and externally becomes extremely important. Buy-in to the big-picture goals can equal support, application of resources, and allocation of time so that you can begin taking the necessary first steps.

Finally, consider the legal implications of your venture. Make sure revenue doesn't "inure" to the benefit of an individual or outside interest, and make sure whatever you do is directly related to the mission of your organization.

Implications for Financial Health

Change is the only constant in today's political and economic climate. You must think strategically about how you can stay afloat, independent of all moorings you may have taken for granted in the past. If done right, forming innovative strategic partnerships will give you the speed, agility, and flexibility to leverage your dollars and achieve your mission, now and in the future.

Chapter 24

Business Planning for Public Health from the North Carolina Institute for Public Health

Stephen N. Orton and Anne J. Menkens

This section of *Managing the Public Health Enterprise* is subtitled "Managing Business," and much of our work at the Management Academy for Public Health is around helping public health managers learn how to write business plans. Dr. Johnson referred to writing a public health business plan in the previous chapter, but what is a public health business plan? And why might you want one?[1]

First, let us discuss why business planning makes sense to today's public health managers. When public health managers conceive of their work as business planning, they begin to graft a business-oriented model of analysis and operation onto the culture of nonprofit and governmental public health. The goal becomes customer service,[2] and the task becomes creating value. It means finding new, different sources of support for programs, diversifying partners, generating revenue, analyzing efficiency, determining cost per unit of service, calculating break even points. If public health were a baseball game (an analogy we use often), creating a successful business plan would be like hitting a grand slam to bring home the resources necessary to improve health in your community.

The shift toward a more entrepreneurial approach to planning social interventions comes in the context of economic uncertainty, rising expectations, and ongoing and emerging health threats. It has

Chapter Source: © 2006 Wolters Kluwer Health | Lippincott Williams & Wilkins. Originally published in *J Public Health Management Practice.* 2006; 12(5): 489–492.

roots in the "reinventing government" movement[3] and the concurrent movement in the nonprofit sector toward social entrepreneurialism.[4–7] Four needs are driving public health ventures in this direction: (1) the need for sustainable financing, (2) for proven results, (3) for improved efficiency, and (4) for effective multisectoral partnerships. Federal and state resources are becoming scarcer and more restrictive; public officials increasingly want demonstrable results for those public funds; grants increasingly require hard outcomes and sustainability plans; and grant funds continue to run in unpredictable cycles, though they are very predictably run out. "Doing more with less" may seem oxymoronic, but the environment requires it.

To sustain public health efforts at the community level, then, managers have to become expert at blending and diversifying funding sources and using those sources as efficiently as possible to achieve outcomes that are both measurable and sustainable. Business planning skills help government speak the language of business—which is increasingly the language of effective nonprofits as well. Many businesses are looking to engage in venture philanthropy and achieve a social return on investment; they are increasingly interested in public health, starting with public health hazards that could impact their bottom line. Taken together, these forces are driving public health managers to analyze and plan for sustainability the way businesses do.

Envisioning sustainability is a mind-set; business planning is a means to that end. Public health planning begins with an idea—a perception of a need in the community and a data-driven strategy to address it. Business planning similarly starts with assessment, always asking the question, "How can I solve this problem in a financially sustainable way?" To answer this question, an entrepreneurial public health manager must first know—in detail—the *feasibility* of the proposed plan. What is the evidence that the plan will work, with limited risk, in a way that is sustainable after the grant ends?

The Feasibility Study

Undertaking a feasibility study will help you begin to think through the practicability of your project. A feasibility study is the first step in business planning, where you look at the data to determine who needs what, you analyze the environment in which you will act, study the relevant models, determine exactly how to measure your success, and ensure the sustainability of your efforts by analyzing the financial picture. A simple feasibility study will help you decide whether to invest time in a full business plan, and it should serve as a blueprint for your business plan. The essential distinction between a feasibility plan and a full business plan is the level of detail. The following are critical components of both.

Narrative Description

You should be able to tell your business plan as a story: this is the problem, and this is the solution. Describe the plan in two or three short paragraphs, in plain language, giving clear answers to key questions about its practicability: Is the project justified by the available needs assessment data? Do you have the resources? Are there models and evidence suggesting plans of this type are effective? Can outcomes be measured effectively? Will it support itself financially? Is it the same old thing, or a creative, fresh, tailored solution? Are the right community partners at the table and committed?

Demonstration of Need and Target Market

Public health managers are experts on the population health needs of their communities. Use the data to show how important a problem is, and who is affected. Describe that data, and convince your audience that the problem is worth solving. Clarify the nature of the gap your plan is intended to fill. Define your target market, and use data to demonstrate need in this particular market. You may need to demonstrate that members of the target group have had some input into the assessment and planning process. Show what need is not being met efficiently or why clients are not benefiting from current services. Compare benefits of funding the project to costs of failing to fund it. Think about tangible and intangible benefits of implementing your project. For example, one team we worked with at the Management Academy for Public Health implemented a plan to involve high school students with teaching younger children about healthy nutrition and active living. Planners found that having a cadre of peer health educators in the school system has gone far beyond peer education to affect the health habits of the larger community.[8] And, another public health department's business plan to fund and build a spay/neuter facility has led to higher customer satisfaction and subsequent higher rates of pet adoption, an unexpected benefit that is in the long run just as important as increasing pet sterilization.[9]

Definition of Plan

Describe the idea in detail. Outline the size and scope of your project, as well as your objectives. What specific services or products or interventions are you planning? What is your client/geographic focus? What is your time line? What are your plan's resource requirements? Are your stated objectives achievable? Carefully work through the many stakeholders involved individually: How will each be affected? Are your stated objectives logical? Are they pointed in the same direction? What are the critical success factors—the one or two things that have to happen for the plan to succeed? For instance, many existing programs provide access to dental care for children in rural communities; what factors do successful plans have in common? Ability to bill Medicaid? Buy-in from dentists? Availability of dental assistants?

Measurement

Describe the health goals you hope to achieve, and plan for data collection that will show progress toward those goals. What improvements in community health status can be expected as a result of your project? What process measures will you track? How will they be measured? How will you know if you have hit a "home run" with your project? Businesses often have very sophisticated ways of tracking performance: not just sales but sales to returning customers, marketing impressions, customer satisfaction, wait times, and return rates. This section of the business plan challenges you to understand deeply the process by which your plan will work to achieve its objectives, and then figure out how to measure it at each step. One public health department we worked with implemented an ambitious plan to provide community-based access to care for the uninsured;[10] process measures such as physician satisfaction and outcomes such as number of patients served were identified as important measures of the program's value and sustainability. Such measurement will add value to the program when its administrators need to attract new partners or sponsors, or affect policy makers, or decide years down the road whether to continue it.

Industry Analysis

We pride ourselves on the extent to which public health is evidence-based, but many businesses are just as "evidence-based" in their planning. Typical business plans include detailed analyses of things like key success factors and life cycle of a particular industry and market niche. Good public health program plans include similar analyses of the latest medical science and the evidence for (and against) specific approaches. Describe the "industry" in which your project fits and what you know about the structure of the industry. Is it a health promotion project? A screening project? Perhaps, as one of our teams did a few years ago,[11] you want to start a program that provides behavioral health care for the underserved. What are the key success factors in the industry? Are there legal, political, regulatory, technological, or economic obstacles to implementing your plan? How will you overcome these barriers? Could partners help?

Competitors/Partners

In the business world, new efforts usually try to escape competitors and instead "run to space." A few decide to confront competitors head-on. In public health, there are plenty of health problems to go around: the goal is generally to describe how your business plan fills a gap in the public health system. You may have competitors: for instance, your plan may encroach upon services offered by local hospitals or other healthcare providers, health clubs, or others. Your plan should describe how your business plan complements and integrates with existing efforts in your organization and in the broader community. Who are the agencies and organizations with interests in this space? Who are the natural community/state/national partners in this project? How does this plan fit with their goals and objectives? Is the local environment receptive to this sort of plan? What is distinctive about your services relative to those of competitors in the marketplace?

Time Line

A detailed listing of key events and specific dates by which they will happen will help you determine the reasonableness of your idea and your needs for finances, personnel, and time. This section becomes a critical part of calculating financial needs in business: you must have enough cash throughout the process to pay the bills. In a world where grants or government allocations often cover start-up costs, initial cash flow is less a concern, but the timeline is critically important for clarifying steps and assigning roles for multiagency or multiorganizational efforts.

Risk and Exit Plan

Launching a program within the government sometimes requires us to soft-pedal the downside and push the upside to legislators and constituents, but experienced public health managers understand the risks and pitfalls of different kinds of interventions. The specific risks for your topic area and organization or community should be listed and analyzed. What are the things that could go wrong, and what preventive measures can be taken? How will you know if the program is not working? How will you shut the program down, if necessary? For public health business plans, exit planning has an added function: planning the transition of a successful program to another entity. For some public health programs, success is defined by the ability of the governmental agencies to smoothly hand off day-to-day operations of an ongoing intervention to organizations in the nonprofit or perhaps even the business sector: to assure services, in other words. Both possible "exits" should be prepared for in the business plan.

Financial Resources

Writing a business plan means seeing money as part of the analytical problem, instead of seeing it as part of the frame. Often in our work, we start with a certain amount of money as a constant: such-and-such foundation or agency wants proposals for how we would spend $500,000 over three years on diabetes prevention. Business plan finance is more dynamic. The task is to balance resources (including cash) and costs, using the best possible assumptions to get the best possible recommendation. To return to the dental care example: How many children can you sign up? How many could you see, given the staffing and space? What services will those children need, and in what proportions? How much will it cost to provide fixed items such as personnel, equipment, and space? How much will it cost to provide service to each child? The revenue side of the equation is similarly complex: Who pays how much for what, when? How many children must you see to break even? What is the estimated five-year budget for your business plan? What will have to happen to make the program sustainable financially in the long term? The dynamic nature of this analysis requires detailed financial projections and assumptions. Public health business plans often use grants to start up an effort, but the best go beyond grants and general fund monies. People who read business plans for a living often start with the finance section. It provides the framework on which the more narrative parts of the plan hang. And the level of detail in this section provides an instant reality check on the assumptions made in the plan. Some signs that your assumptions may be flawed:

- A nurse is funded half time—to run a screening program that will triple in size over three years.
- The Public Health Department is providing a big chunk of the required resources as in-kind donations of staff time— forever, without new hires.
- Monthly expenses are the same every month—for a program to deliver influenza shots in schools.

Your finance section will give an early indication of sustainability. Does the program rely on a grant to come through in the future, or an existing grant to get extended? Do the revenue projections require unrealistically large utilization rates or market penetration? Does the program allocate money for evaluation? Are there agreements in place with partners who are donating critical resources such as space and equipment? Have you accounted for in-kind contributions?

The Business Plan

When you have answered the questions above, you have essentially begun writing a business plan for a new initiative that addresses a need in your community. You will need a business plan if (1) your sponsors or political allies (or foes!) want to see one; (2) your partners want to see one; or (3) you want to generate revenue. In short, if you want to implement your initiative and do so in a sustainable way, you need a business plan. A major difference between feasibility studies and business plans is that the former asks questions and the latter makes statements on the basis of the answers to those questions. A *business plan* is an argument that a new venture *should* be done and *can* be done; it sells the idea, and your capacity to execute it. It also prepares an important road map for action that is useful to you and your potential partners and supporters. Business plans are not for internal projects, such as creating a new human resources manual, but are for external, revenue-generating projects.

Business plans are not for doing strategic planning but for executing existing strategies: they are concrete implementation plans within the broader strategic plans of organizations and communities. And although business plans are designed to sell ideas, you should not use them to sell yourself on a bad idea. Business plans are meant to help predict a future outcome with as much certainty as possible.

Business plans that succeed are often *testable* (you could do a pilot version); *reversible* (can return to status quo); *divisible* (can be implemented in stages); *concrete* (with tangible results); *supported* (cover sunk costs, building on existing programs and resources); *familiar* (models are available); *congruent* (match goals, initiatives); *widely valued* (have publicity value that stakeholders will appreciate); *marginal* (not risky to the complete enterprise); *idiosyncratic* (you can start it by yourself); and *timely* (reacts to an emerging crisis or uses a new means of attacking an old problem). Many business plans do not succeed. Good business planning can prevent those failures from being catastrophic.

References

1. For a more detailed discussion of how to write a public health business plan, see Orton S, Menkens A, and Santos P. *Public Health Business Planning: A Practical Guide.* Sudbury, MA: Jones and Bartlett Publishers, 2008 and www.publichealthbusiness planning.org

2. Barzelay M. *Breaking through Bureaucracy: A New Vision for Managing in Government.* Berkeley: University of California Press; 1992.

3. Osborne D, Gaebler T. *Reinventing Government: How the Entrepreneurial Spirit Is Transforming the Public Sector.* Reading, MA: Addison-Wesley; 1992.

4. Bornstein D. *The Price of a Dream.* Chicago, IL: University of Chicago Press; 1996.

5. Bornstein D. *How to Change the World: Social Entrepreneurs and the Power of New Ideas.* New York, NY: Oxford University Press; 2004.

6. Dees G, Emerson J, Economy P. *Enterprising Nonprofits: A Toolkit for Social Entrepreneurs.* New York, NY: John Wiley & Sons; 2001.

7. Dees G, Emerson J, Economy P. *Strategic Tools for Social Entrepreneurs: Enhancing the Performance of Your Enterprising Nonprofit.* New York, NY: John Wiley & Sons; 2002.

8. Thomas AB, Ward E. Peer power: how Dare County, North Carolina, is addressing chronic disease through innovative programming. *J Public Health Manage Pract.* 2006;12(5):462–467.

9. McNeil J, Constandy E. Addressing the problem of pet overpopulation: the experience of New Hanover County Animal Control Services. *J Public Health Manage Pract.* 2006;12(5):452–455.

10. Scotten ESL, Absher AC. Creating community-based access to primary health-care for the uninsured through strategic alliances and restructuring local health department programs. *J Public Health Manage Pract.* 2006;12(5):446–451.

11. Mims S. A sustainable behavioral health program integrated with public health primary care. *J Public Health Manage Pract.* 2006;12(5):456–461.

12. For more information about the Management Academy for Public Health, visit www.maph.unc.edu

Chapter 25

Business Process Improvement: Working Smarter, Not Harder

Tracy Lockard

Public Health and Business Processes

You may have heard the expression that "if you have *seen one* public health department you've *seen only one* public health department," meaning that all public health departments are unique and operate differently. When the Robert Wood Johnson Foundation (www.rwjf.org) developed the national program *Common Ground: Transforming Public Health Information Systems*, one of its goals was for state and local public health departments across the country to collaborate in defining and improving business processes by documenting our work clearly and using that information to adopt, implement, and endorse redesigned business processes and requirements definitions for information systems to support the work of public health.

Many times when public health staff is asked about their business processes, they do not think they have "business" processes, since the job of public health is to care for people and protect the health of the population. If they do think of a business process, they usually focus on the financial aspects of the health department, such as the budget process. A *business process* describes a set of activities and tasks that logically group together to accomplish a goal or produce something of value for the benefit of the organization, stakeholder, or customer. Business processes frequently cut across departmental and organizational boundaries.

173

Every department in public health has business processes, such as appointment scheduling, clinical visits, food and lodging inspections, hiring employees, and insurance billing. By evaluating public health business processes and working collaboratively, public health agencies can make improvements in service delivery, quality, and performance, and the goal of doing more with less can be reached.

Through the Common Ground grant awarded to the Cabarrus Health Alliance, the Public Health Authority of Cabarrus County, in 2006, over 100 public health leaders from several regional health departments in the Southern Piedmont Partnership for Public Health have learned the skills of business process analysis and the benefits of collaboration in planning and refining business processes. As part of this grant, Cabarrus Health Alliance applied a methodology developed by the Public Health Informatics Institute, the national program office for Common Ground. The Institute's Requirements Development Methodology builds on many standard business methodologies but is unique in that it is tailored to the public health environment and applies a collaborative approach, bringing stakeholders and agencies together to define the way tasks are conducted, to identify opportunities for improvement, and ultimately to develop requirements for the optimal information solution.

The Steps of Requirements Development Methodology

The first step in business process improvement is business process analysis. The three tools used in this analysis are (1) the business process matrix, (2) the context diagram, and (3) the task-flow diagram. In combination, these three tools comprehensively describe how work is currently done. The business process matrix focuses on higher-level attributes of a business process, such as the goals, objectives, and business rules. The context diagram focuses on who (person or computer system) is involved in the business process and what information they exchange. Last, the task-flow diagram focuses on the sequence of tasks performed to carry out the process. Similar to the work-flow diagram frequently used in business, the task-flow diagram shows who (job title or job descriptor) is carrying out each task, which is extremely beneficial when evaluating workload.

Business process analysis focuses on *current* activities; business process redesign focuses on how work *should* be done by examining ways to create more effective and efficient processes. A good starting point for examining business processes is a review of those tasks where data are entered multiple times, tasks are duplicated, or where the process is not standardized. Any time someone says, "This is the way we've always done it," this usually screams for closer examination and redesign of the business process. Basically, business process redesign is a process of identifying and eliminating non-value-added tasks that add waste and complexity to the process. Beyond identifying and eliminating inefficient activities, measurement is another critical part of implementing changes and conducting quality improvement. Measures show differences in performance when a business process is changed and tell you whether the changes you make actually lead to improvement.

Requirements definition, the last step in business process improvement, focuses on describing what the information system must do to help with the work. Of course, some processes within public health do not require information systems, but those that do must have their requirements defined. An information system should work the way you want it to work, not add to your workload. Especially if you are transitioning from primarily a paper-driven process to an electronic system, the last thing you want to do is automate a bad process. Using subject-matter experts who understand information technology, as well as staff who understand the basic and advanced system requirements, will allow you to define the information system that will handle your needs now and in the future.

Applying Business Process Improvement to a Public Health Initiative

The Southern Piedmont Partnership for Public Health has seen the value of performing business process analysis and redesign in a collaborative project. In preparation for the North Carolina Department of Public Health's release of a new Health Information System, staff from seven health departments and consultants from the Department of Public Health worked together to analyze business processes within family planning, child health, and billing, all of which would change drastically under the new system. Each health department had different objectives in undertaking the project. For example, some of the health departments involved wanted to increase the likelihood of a smooth transition from the current state system to the new system. Other health departments wanted to understand the business processes to develop requirements with which to evaluate the new system as well as other practice management/electronic medical record systems.

And other health departments wanted to gather requirements for future enhancements to the new system, such as the electronic exchange of medical record data with a provider or other health information network. Although the objectives were different, the process of analyzing and revaluating business processes and defining requirements was the same.

Knowing that the new Health Information System would require significant business process changes, especially in the clinical assessment and billing areas, the team worked collaboratively to develop best practice work flows and to determine recommendations for computer systems and networks. Subject-matter experts from each health department analyzed and discussed their business processes, discovering that the health departments actually had many similarities. Subject-matter experts shared how current processes and procedures were performed, thus getting a head start on the redesign phase. From listening and discussing the business processes with their colleagues, team members found ways to make their current processes more efficient and effective.

To assist in the statewide rollout of the Health Information System, the team took the analysis and redesign of the family planning, child health, and billing business processes one step further. They evaluated the prerelease version of the system and added to the task-flow diagrams the specific menu path in the new system that is used to perform the task. Many of the tasks were previously performed manually. The task-flow diagrams became an effective training tool for the various users of the new system as well as a best practice work flow for the new Health Information System. In addition, by evaluating the prerelease version of the system and the redesigned task-flow diagrams, the team could capture enhancements for future releases of the Health Information System as well as business decisions that each health department needed to consider before going live with the new system.

Health departments evaluating other practice management/electronic medical record system options had to analyze business processes within other areas of the health department that would be affected by a new information system. Planners from these departments collaboratively analyzed and redesigned their business practices and developed requirements for these areas: billing, child health, communicable disease, family planning, intensive home visiting, lab, maternal care coordination/child services coordination, maternal health, and medical records. On the basis of the features and functionality requirements determined by the business process analysis and redesign phase, each health department independently evaluated which software application best met its needs.

When it was time to evaluate the various software applications, in addition to watching typical sales demonstration presentations, team members gave vendors impromptu test cases with real world public health business process scenarios to see how closely the different systems fit the best practice task flows developed by the team. The team visited vendors' clients currently using the software to see the applications in action and learn about pitfalls encountered by users. Tools such as checklists to compare vendors and a scoring system allowed for an unbiased analysis of the vendors. Subject-matter experts that represented all departments affected by a new system were integral members of the team, involved throughout the process of selecting and recommending an information system that would best meet the needs of the public health department. This collaboration and involvement aided in the ownership and adoption of the new system by staff.

Business process analysis, redesign, and requirements definition require facilitators with strong project management skills and subject-matter experts for the specific business process. The process described here required a significant amount of time and resources; however, practice management/electronic medical record software has a great impact on the daily workings of a local public health department. The technology chosen will likely be used for the next 15 or more years, therefore requiring a thorough analysis before a sound decision can be made.

Public health departments need to fully understand their business processes and how these business processes may be supported and enhanced through new technology. The Public Health Informatics Institute's Requirements Development Methodology is an efficient way for large or small local public health departments or state public health departments to document and define their work. The methodology provides steps for the development of a thorough features and functionality document to help make well-informed strategic decisions much easier for stakeholders. This collaboration yields a sound foundation for managing the scope and planning for the implementation of a new system.

Conclusion

The importance of business process improvement projects goes far beyond preparing for new large-scale information systems. Collaborating on this type of analysis and documenting the results allows health departments to gain a better understanding of their own business processes and of how other health departments approach these processes. Also, the documentation of task-flow diagrams is an especially useful training tool for new employees and a reference tool for managers. New employees can see how their tasks fit into the process, see whom they will interact with, and see the bigger picture of the work they perform. Managers can examine the documented business processes in conjunction with time studies and other metrics to see where bottlenecks are occurring and to help balance workloads. Quality improvement work, both at the individual and at the organizational level, involves examining your business processes and measuring the impact to determine whether change works.

Common Ground grantees from across the country applied the methodology to work within their own organization and collaboratively applied the methodology to define a set of business processes related to chronic diseases and public health preparedness. Working together to share ideas and resources to describe the work of public health, the grantees were able to accomplish more than they would have if they had worked separately. Their development of the features and functionality requirements for an information system for chronic disease and public health preparedness business processes formed the basis for a set of requirements that can be customized by a broad range of users. Other state and local public health departments, not involved in the analysis, will benefit from this work by being able to focus their attention on customizing features to meet their specific local needs.

In every area of planning, it is important to determine your needs up front. Using process analysis and redesign to develop requirements for business processes is a systematic approach to defining organizational needs. Such a systematic, planned approach is necessary for success. Designing an information system that can work more efficiently and effectively now will pay for itself in the long run. If other business processes within the health department are streamlined to work with information systems, you will save time and money. Without a planned approach, improvements to a business process that involves an information system are more costly to develop and to deploy. Remember, "Failure to plan is planning to fail."

For more information on the Public Health Informatics Institute's Requirements Development Methodology, visit http://www.phii.org/resources/doc/Taking_Care_of_Business.pdf

Chapter 26

Fundraising 101: Why Seek Private Funding?

Gregory Philip Duyck

G overnmental public health managers often grapple with a stark and unpleasant reality: demand for their programs, services, time, and talent usually outstrips supply. In addition, the primary resource used to increase supply—tax-based funding from local, state, and federal governments—faces constant downward pressure that constricts its flow to public health agencies.

In this context, access to private funding sources becomes increasingly important. Raising money may seem alien and yet another burden in an already endless day. Taken up seriously, however, fund development can be a critical resource in serving your clients. As a fundraiser for both public agencies and private nonprofits, as well as a former development officer at one of the largest community foundations in the country, I have seen all sides of the private funding equation. This chapter will explore why public health managers should include fundraising as a part of their revenue-generating activities and what to consider before entering into development.

One initial piece of advice: do not focus on individuals. It would be great if Bill Gates walked into your agency and fell in love with your outstanding staff and remarkable programs, but this is unlikely. Building a successful individual giving program is a costly, long-term endeavor, especially for an agency without a natural donor constituency (i.e., alumni, grateful patients, parishioners, or membership base).

Chapter Source: © 2008 Wolters Kluwer Health | Lippincott Williams & Wilkins. Originally published in J *Public Health Management Practice.* 2008; 14(2): 199–201.

While individuals accounted for more than 83% of all private giving in the United States in 2006,[1] the vast majority of these funds go to organizations that have that built-in constituency, including churches, museums, educational institutions, and healthcare organizations.

This leaves two other private sources: foundations and corporations. Foundations are private or community-based grant-making institutions that fund projects, often in particular areas defined by the organization's founder staff and board of directors. A corporation, of course, is a for-profit business. Foundations and corporations can be local, national, or international in scope, and they have unique cultures that present challenges to development. It will take hours of work to understand those cultures and seek the support you want, possibly to no avail. But there are many reasons to explore this brave new world:

1. *Better programs.* The development process often forces organizations to analyze their programs more deeply and plan for them more carefully. This effort will lead to effective outcomes, including partnerships with other agencies, better use of staff and resources, and sometimes even the rational abandonment of a flawed idea.

2. *Wider outreach.* A relationship with a knowledgeable funder plugs your agency into a network of organizations that can improve your initiatives and expand their reach. Just as you are an expert in your community's population health, program officers at foundations and corporations are experts in the nonprofit sector. They often know about services in the community similar to those proposed by applicants and can suggest potential partners in a new venture. A grant will also raise the profile of a program or an agency, providing invaluable public relations for its work.

3. *Fewer restrictions on funds.* Restriction, in this case, has two meanings. First, corporate and some small foundation grants often come with fewer constraints than federal funds and other government grants. This allows grantees great flexibility. Second, for those grant makers that fund in a specific discipline or for a specific purpose, you can often define the "restrictions" yourself. For example, if a funder is interested only in supporting community-based HIV prevention programs, an agency can decide to apply for support of a staff person, outreach materials, the Web site needed to market the program, or a summit of HIV service providers to develop a comprehensive program.

4. *You can't win if you don't play.* All private foundations must, by law, distribute a portion of their assets each year for grant-making

programs. Corporations depend on grants to generate goodwill and positive public relations in their communities. By starting a development effort, you can access these dollars and begin building relationships with grant makers who, every year, seek worthy grantees to implement quality programs. The longer your positive relationship with a funder, the more trusted you are and the more likely you will receive the next grant you seek.

Seeking private support is clearly worthwhile, but there are a number of issues to consider before pressing ahead. Public health agencies enjoy distinct advantages in seeking funding from private funders as well as some disadvantages that must be dispelled or minimized to be successful.

Advantages

1. *Stability.* An agency that is publicly funded enjoys an institutional stability that no nonprofit can match. Barring a dramatic shift in public policy, your agency will continue to provide public health services no matter what. Funders value agency sustainability, so emphasize it. In addition, government funding streams provide an infrastructure of office space, personnel, phone service, and other basics, while nonprofits must renew their sources of revenue for these expenses each year.
2. *Data mastery.* Data gathering and analysis infuse the public health culture, and public health agencies are recognized experts in population health. In fact, North Carolina and many other states require community health assessments that gather critical data. Public health agencies can use these data to demonstrate clear need for a new program as they begin discussions with grant makers and use the data-gathering mechanisms already in place to create solid evaluation plans. Many funders require both and are becoming more stringent in their assessments of these components.
3. *Access to state and federal revenue streams.* While much support from government funders is tied to specific programs, public health managers may also know about discretionary funding that nonprofits cannot access. Leveraging these dollars by seeking complementary private support pleases corporate and foundation funders and creates stronger programs. Also, public funders now often expect or reward agencies that can attract private support to the programs they fund. Every grant maker—public or private—wants to support sustainable programs.

Disadvantages

1. *Public entities are sometimes excluded from funding.* A real barrier to applying for foundation and corporate funds is a prohibition by some grant makers against supporting public agencies. They believe that taxpayers should support these organizations. If you partner with a nonprofit organization on a project, this prohibition can be circumvented by making the partner the applicant organization.
2. *Misconception that government agencies do not innovate.* Some program officers may labor under the fallacy that your agency spends all of its time and resources implementing mandated programs. Know ahead of time that a large part of your fundraising effort will be to educate funders about your work and creative programming.
3. *Budgetary restrictions.* While public health agencies have the freedom to develop innovative programs, initiatives mandated and funded by the local, state, or federal government compose a significant portion of their portfolios. Use this to your advantage by showing that you are the most important or a very important player in the areas in which you work. Your status as a public agency increases your credibility.

In any proposal to a foundation or corporation, remind the reader of your advantages and directly address the disadvantages. Anticipate negative misconceptions and demonstrate your knowledge of your community's public health challenges.

Tips for Moving Forward

In addition to understanding their own agency and how it is perceived, public health managers considering grant seeking must also understand the nature of private grant making. In my years of seeking funds from and working for funders, I have identified a few parameters for seeking private grants:

1. *Think globally, ask locally.* The closer an agency's proximity to a grant maker, the higher the likelihood of funding. You would be right to think that Exxon has a lot of money to give away. But the 1.7 million nonprofits in the United States[2] as well as all of the governmental units that are also beginning to seek grants are thinking the same thing. Moreover, unless your agency is close

to Exxon's Irving, Texas, headquarters or a major Exxon facility, the likelihood of being funded is very low. A quote from their corporate-giving Web site says it simply: "While we generally prefer to invest in communities where we have a strong local presence, we also fund some organizations that operate across a nation or around the globe."[3] Exxon funds only a few organizations—and only those with a national or international footprint—outside its operating areas. Especially if your programs are primarily local in nature, find local grant makers to fund them. They are invested in the outcome because their staff and board live in your community, too.

2. *Expect short-term funding.* Even if you focus on local corporations and foundations, you still face stiff competition. Because the needs of every community are so great, an individual funder is bombarded each year with dozens, and in many cases hundreds, of applications. Juxtaposed with this stack of proposals is the relatively small amount of money funders give away. Given this ratio, corporations and foundations generally adopt a practice of providing only short-term funding to grantees so that they can support a greater number of nonprofits. You should plan for 1 to 3 years of funding from a single source bridging to long-term, self-sustaining revenue generation after that.

3. *Grant makers reward innovation.* Most private funders seek proposals that create groundbreaking programs or expand innovative initiatives with a record of success. Specifically, they would like to support new projects with clear, measurable goals that can be assessed within the grant-making period.

4. *Ask for ornaments and not the tree.* While seeking proposals for new or expanding programs, corporations and foundations generally shy away from funding operating or capital expenditures. In general, they do not want to fund infrastructure; they would prefer exciting initiatives with definable objectives. Some grant makers—generally small foundations or corporations making gifts from marketing or other budgets—will make a general gift to an organization. These gifts, however, are usually small. While operating costs may be your greatest need, focus fundraising efforts on program support.

5. *Know the funder's motivation.* Before you submit the application to a funder, consider your audience.

   ▪ A foundation is in the business of making good grants that change the world in a positive way by addressing critical needs. Emphasize in your proposal the need you are addressing and how *exactly* your program meets that need. Foundation staff and board members are motivated by improvement in the community—ensure your program makes a measurable improvement and your proposal states clearly how it will occur.

■ A corporation is in the business of generating profit and pleasing a variety of stakeholders—politicians, employees, board members, and customers. For this reason, the public relations value of your innovative, new program should be clearly emphasized. Not all corporations seek public relations value in return for their grant dollars, but few would turn it down. When thinking about a corporate funder, consider a project or an aspect of a larger project that has recognizable impact that can be documented.

These tips are only broad-brush suggestions and do not represent the philosophies of individual funders. My goal is to provide an overall view of this landscape. Fundraising may be new territory, but there are many reasons to explore it and much for you to gain for your agency and your clients. And, development may not be as foreign as you imagine. The quickest way to understand fundraising is to consider your own philanthropy. If you make gifts to charities, you probably reserve your largest ones for the organizations you know best while making small investments in nonprofits you believe in but have not connected with deeply. The same can be said for grant makers— the relationship is the key.

In the following two chapters, I will go beyond the *why* of fundraising to more specific tips about *how* to prepare for and begin raising funds from foundations and corporations.

References

1. The Center on Philanthropy at Indiana University. *Giving USA* 2007. Indianapolis, IN: Giving USA Foundation; 2006.

2. Internal Revenue Service. Tax-exempt organization and other entities listed on the exempt organization business master file, by type of organization and internal revenue code section, fiscal years 2003–2006. In: *Internal Revenue Service Data Book* 2006. Available at: http://www.irs.gov/pub/irs-soi/06databk.pdf. Accessed November 30, 2007.

3. http://www.exxonmobil.com/Corporate/community_contributions.aspx. Accessed December 3, 2007.

27

Fundraising 101: Getting Started

Gregory Philip Duyck

It is fun to imagine sitting in the waiting area of a corporate office on the top floor of a soaring skyscraper with multiple copies of a handsome, full-color funding proposal in hand that explains exactly why that company should support your agency for the next five years. Or, to picture yourself sitting in the quiet boardroom of a large private foundation, admiring the art on the walls as you wait to talk with a friendly program officer, a laptop humming beside you with a concise and persuasive PowerPoint presentation that clearly elucidates why the foundation should become the lead donor for your groundbreaking project. It is even more fun to imagine that, as you wait, you are completely confident that you will achieve these outcomes.

But how to get there? In the previous chapter, I discussed some of the reasons that a public health agency might want to raise private funds as well as some things to consider before choosing this path. In this chapter, I will describe steps necessary to prepare you and your agency to raise support from corporations and foundations.

Develop Agency Priorities

If you wish to create a successful corporate and foundation fundraising program, you would do well to remember an old saw: "If you fail

Chapter Source: © 2008 Wolters Kluwer Health | Lippincott Williams & Wilkins. Originally published in *J Public Health Management Practice.* 2008; 14(4): 407–409.

to plan, you plan to fail." Ideally, you have a strategic plan that identifies your agency's priorities for fulfilling its responsibilities over the short term and long term. These responsibilities include activities mandated and funded by your state or local government, but you should also consider how discretionary initiatives may support your organizational goals as well. It is these discretionary initiatives that provide the opportunity to raise private support.

Developing your agency's overall priorities demonstrates to a foundation or a corporation that you are serious and thoughtful about the direction your organization is taking and a contributor's potential role in it. Donors give to programs that move an organization forward and help accomplish a mission that aligns with the donor's own philanthropic goals. To understand this concept, think of your own philanthropy. If you are asked to give a sacred object to your church's new sanctuary, you would like to know how it would serve the growing congregation. If asked to give to a homeless shelter, you would like to know how the organization is coping with homelessness in the long term. The larger the gift, the more this is true. Major donors want to know how their money will be used. Beginning the fundraising process with organizational priorities is crucial.

The priorities you adopt should reflect your agency's strengths and the challenges faced by your community. They will be different for every organization. An agency may want to reduce obesity or improve water quality or design a comprehensive emergency preparedness plan. Whatever you decide, ensure that the entire organization is committed to these goals and that they are possible to accomplish.*

Develop Fundable Projects to Meet Priorities

Once you have established your agency's priorities, create projects with the potential to receive private support that will help you reach organizational objectives. If, for example, your priority is to reduce obesity in your community, first research the literature to determine what approaches have been effective:

- Educating the general population about healthy food choices.
- Starting neighborhood-based walking clubs with a nutrition education component.

---

*For a comprehensive look at strategic planning for public health, see the special issue devoted to the public health planning tool MAPP, Mobilizing for Action through Planning and Partnerships. J Public Health Manage Pract. 2005;11(5).

- Targeting students with nutrition and exercise information that will spread virally to their families.
- Combining these or other approaches.

Use your skills at analyzing programs to identify the best approach for your community to adopt, then commit to finding the funding for it.

What type of program will appeal to corporate and foundation donors? Development officers talk about the latest trends in grant making or "buzz words" that should be included in any proposal. However, if an organization builds the best program in its community to accomplish a goal, it will find a funder. Certainly take care to make your venture understandable to your audience, but to most donors—and especially institutional donors—a fundable project is one that *works*. The agency might not find all the support the program needs to thrive, and the program may not succeed in the long run. But most of the time, a great idea coupled with the right approach will find champions.

Develop a Plan for Funding Your Program

Once you have a program you believe will succeed, break the project down into smaller chunks that can be funded by a variety of sources. Here, agency leadership must take a long, hard look at its own finances and revenue to find sources of support that can be coupled with private donations to fund a new venture. If an organization is able to find other funding sources, the donor's confidence increases greatly as does the likelihood of a gift. Donors prefer not to be sole funders of significant programs for a number of reasons:

- Other revenue sources spread the risk around.
- Broad support in the community indicates better chances of success.
- The donor has limited resources and may wish to limit his or her gift to the program.

Of course, there are exceptions. If a donor is approached to make a gift to a building on a college campus, he or she may want to make the gift exclusively to obtain recognition in the form of his or her name on the structure. But in the case of programs or initiatives, especially new ones, donors prefer funding partners.

Sources that you could review for possible funding include the following:

- Your agency's own funds (even if a small amount).

- Personnel time or other agency in-kind contributions.
- State funds available for the type of program you are creating.
- Local partners that could cost-share with you (e.g., a hospital that could lend a nutritionist to develop obesity reduction materials or educate the public about the risks of obesity).

This list will pain many readers. You may be asking, "If I had the money for the program, why would I need private support?" This is a reasonable question, but look at the donor as an investor. An investor does not want to be the only one taking the risk for a program—especially a new program developed by an organization that probably has not received a gift or grant from that investor before. Also, you look stronger if you attract other funders, and you can bet that the nonprofits who are your stiffest competition for the grant will include additional funding sources in their proposals.

One more point. Although you cannot predict whether all the revenue sources that you outline in the grant will come through, you must make a good faith effort to secure them. You cannot forecast whether you will receive a state grant, for example, or know that a partner will absolutely join your initiative. But if they do not, you will have to explain why when reporting back to the funder. Focus on realistic funding sources for your new initiatives and try very hard to obtain them.[1]

Identify Prospects

The final step in building the foundation for a private fundraising program is to identify prospects that are likely to support your initiatives. As with most aspects of fundraising, this process begins with those who are closest to the agency and moves out from there:

1. *Previous donors.* If you have received grants or gifts from corporations or foundations, these past donors are your best prospects for future contributions. Start your list here.
2. *Friends of the agency.* These could be program officers from local foundations you have met while sitting on task forces or local boards, members of a community advisory council you have put together for a grant, or the spouse of one of your staff members who has an executive position at a local corporation. These individuals' knowledge of your organization's past work will help convince them to support you going forward.

3. *Vendors to the agency.* These could be medical supply vendors to your free clinic or the supplier of the vaccine you use for free shots. Be creative and think about where your organization spends most of its budget. There should not be a quid pro quo relationship, but there is no reason not to approach vendors to consider giving to the same program or agency from which they are profiting.

4. *Local businesses or foundations.* These organizations are more likely to have heard about you and your good work than organizations working three states away. When compiling your list, think of the largest local businesses and foundations as well as national companies with local plants or work sites.

5. *Funder directories.* After you have exhausted the options outlined here, it may be time to do some research in a directory of funding sources. There may be a good, local directory of institutional donors. Calling your local Association of Fundraising Professionals chapter should yield this answer. If there is not one, the *Foundation Center Directory* is the most comprehensive national database of corporate and foundation contributors.

Research using a funder directory warrants additional comments. These compilations can be accessed at a local library, and a reference librarian can help navigate the electronic or print version. Focus your search on funders who target your state or community for their funding. It is highly unlikely that a corporation or foundation with a nationwide grant-making program would be interested in supporting a local initiative.* Also, target only funders who give to the discipline area of your program (i.e., health programs if you are developing an obesity reduction initiative). Do not waste your time on funders who "should" be interested in your organization—just find those who are.

It is not essential—or even possible sometimes—to complete each of these steps before launching a fundraising program. But taking these steps will ensure the best program for your agency in the long run. In the next chapter, we will move beyond fundraising preparation to execution.

---

*There are exceptions to the local funder rule, like the National Association of County and City Health Officials (NACCHO), which offers small grants to public health agencies. But these national organizations attract many applicants, so an individual agency's chances of winning a grant from them are relatively low.

Reference

1. Orton SN, Menkens AJ, and Santos P. *Public Health Business Planning: A Practical Guide.* Sudbury, MA: Jones and Bartlett Publishers; 2007:7. Chapter 10, "Competitors and Partners" is especially good on how and why to develop partnerships.

Chapter 28

Fundraising 101: Executing Your Plan

Gregory Philip Duyck

The difference between understanding fundraising and actually raising money is like the difference between a parent on Christmas Eve and the same parent on Christmas Day. After the kids have gone to bed, an anxious and sleepy father or mother sits in the living room staring at a thousand pieces of an army fort or a tricycle or a dollhouse without much confidence that these parts will yield a suitable, Santa-delivered gift in the morning. But by the next day, the children are ecstatic, the tricycle rolls, and the parent reaps the reward of the hard work of execution, even if it took until 4:00 a.m.

Fundraising is similar. You may have all the pieces, but how do you put them together to obtain the prize your agency needs? In the previous chapter, I outlined some of the preparatory steps a public health agency would take to develop a fundraising program. These covered the spectrum from establishing agency priorities to identifying possible funding sources. Now, I'll describe how you and your agency can execute your plan and begin raising funds from corporations and foundations.

Chapter Source: © 2008 Wolters Kluwer Health | Lippincott Williams & Wilkins. Originally published in *J Public Health Management Practice.* 2008; 14(6): 608–610.

Engage Funders Directly

I taught a session of Grantwriting 101 to a group of nonprofit professionals once who wanted to learn more about the grant-seeking process. I enjoy teaching, and most of the evaluations reflected this with positive comments about the content and the presentation. I haven't forgotten one negative evaluation, however, because (1) I'm human, and (2) it illustrated a key misunderstanding of some novice fundraisers about the grant-writing process. To paraphrase, the evaluation's author asked me, "Why didn't you tell us how to write proposals?"

Raising money from private sources has more to do with the relationship the development officer or agency professional builds with the funder than with the proposal. That relationship should always be businesslike, and it could span just a single, significant conversation about your project. But the connections you make with potential funders are essential to the success of your fundraising program. Funders are busy and harried, but you must educate them and involve them in your work before they will take an interest in it. That's what I taught in Grantwriting 101.

The first step in building a connection is to understand the funder. After you've identified suitable sources of support through contacts and research, you should request the annual report and grant-making guidelines from each of these organizations. If a corporation or foundation doesn't publish these documents or offers too little information, use the Internet and funder directories at your local library to determine what kinds of grants the organization makes. Learn as much as you can.

Then you should call the funder on the phone. Find out who the right target is—whether it's a program officer at a foundation or a corporate giving officer at a company—and call him or her to discuss your program. You may have to be persistent to reach the right person, but this persistence is worth the effort. If you are professional and cordial, most grant-making staff will be very honest with you about their organization's interest in your project. Writing down questions ahead of time helps keep the conversation moving, and thanking the program officer afterward is essential. If it's feasible, invite the program officer to your agency for an in-depth discussion.

One piece of advice: choose one project to discuss with the contact. When calling a foundation or corporation, a fundraiser will always provide some key background information about his or her agency, but a good one will move quickly to one project selected ahead of time to discuss with the funder. That project will be chosen based on the interests of the grant maker, not on the need of the agency. If the program officer adamantly rejects this project, always have a second one ready to discuss, assuming this idea also fits the grant maker's guidelines. When discussing the agency as a whole, stick to superlatives (e.g., the highest number of uninsured clients of any city clinic or most vaccine inoculations in the state). The program officer will be more likely to remember these.

Your initial conversation with the grant maker will probably focus on the project you would like funded, and that's a good place to start. But you should use this interaction to launch other ways of engaging the program officer in your work: an invitation to your next health fair, a request to serve on a task force in his or her area of expertise, or simply a tour of your facilities. These kinds of activities usually occur out of the grant cycle but are imperative in building a long-term relationship.

Create a Successful Proposal

A conversation with a funder will often yield excellent information. Sometimes the best data you will receive is that the grant maker simply isn't interested in your agency or project. Listen carefully to that response. Many fundraisers continue to blindly pursue grant makers because they feel the funders *should* like their programs. My advice is to move on to other prospects who actually *do* like your program.

Other information you can glean includes how to refine your idea to better fit the funder's guidelines, upcoming deadlines, the general grant range, and whether a foundation or corporation will fund a public agency. All this information and more can help you shape your written proposal so that it's more likely to be funded. Using this data, the next step normally is to write a letter of intent (LOI). This is a short (keep it to two pages) letter describing your agency and the project that you send to your contact. A typical outline of an LOI is the following:

- *1st paragraph*: Introduction and request
- *2nd–4th paragraphs*: Organization background and need for project
- *5th–7th paragraphs*: Project description
- *8th paragraph*: Impact of the project; make the request again
- *9th paragraph*: Close and include phone number

Often, the foundation or corporation will have specific guidelines for the LOI that you should follow to the letter. Funders have established these rules for a purpose, and you would do well to honor them. I suggest that you follow up after submitting the LOI to ensure the grant maker received it and to answer any questions the program officer might have.

For those organizations without specific guidelines, you have more latitude and should take advantage of it. This doesn't mean writing more than two pages; it means being more persistent in your follow-up. If the program officer hasn't visited your agency, call again after submitting the LOI to ensure that it was received and to extend the invitation again. If this invitation is declined, ask if you can meet at his or her office to discuss the project in more depth. Ask about next steps. Don't be rude, but know that program officers are accustomed to persistent agency staff and that you shouldn't be shy.

The turnaround time for an LOI is usually six weeks or so. Sometimes, less formal grant makers make a final decision based on the LOI. If you are funded, congratulations! Go celebrate. If your LOI is not funded or if you aren't asked to complete a full proposal, be sure to follow up with your contact to find out why you were turned down and how you could improve your proposal next time.

If you're asked to submit a full proposal, you've also succeeded. You've just made it through the first screen a grant maker uses to eliminate those they do not wish to fund, and you have the opportunity to dazzle the funder. An agency is usually given a significant period of time to complete the full proposal (6 to 8 weeks), but it is never enough. Organize yourself and your team early and stick to a plan. Key steps include outlining the components of the proposal, drawing up a time line for completing the proposal, pulling together resources such as budget help and administrative support, and confirming external collaborators. Once those steps are taken, attack the proposal using the following guideline and questions:

- *Executive summary*: In one page maximum, summarize each of the six areas that follow.
- *Need for program*: What need in your client population or community must be met?
- *Objectives and impact*: What overall impact will you make on this need? What specific objectives do you hope to accomplish with your program?
- *Strategies and tasks*: How will your program work? How will you achieve your objectives? What specific activities will you initiate to implement the program? How will you achieve the overall impact?
- *Personnel*: Who will oversee this project? What are their credentials? Who will implement this project? What are their credentials?

- *Evaluation*: How will you assess the effectiveness of this project? Specifically, what quantitative and qualitative measures will you use to determine whether you have been successful?
- *Budget*: What are the line-by-line costs for this project, including administrative? Who will fund which parts? Has another funder already committed funds to the project? Are you or a donor contributing in-kind costs to the project?

As with the LOI, follow up with a phone call to ensure the funder received your proposal. If site visits are a part of the standard grant review procedures for this particular grant maker, then wait for that to occur. If not, ask again whether the program officer would be willing to come to your agency and see your work up close. Engaging the foundation or corporation on this personal level is essential, so continue to be persistent even after the grant review process is over.

If your proposal is funded, congratulations! Either way, call the program officer after you learn the outcome to find out how you could improve your project or your proposal the next time. This shows how much you care about being a good grantee. Also, regardless of the outcome, you must continue to engage the funder in your work using the cultivation ideas discussed earlier and others you design. If you make it to the proposal stage, it is a clear indication that the foundation or corporation is interested in your work, and your agency should continue to involve the funder in it.

This engagement is especially important if you are funded. Make sure the director of your agency sends a thank-you note to the program officer after the grant is received. Send requested reports on time and additional reports on progress if you have good news to share. Continue to invite the program officer, other staff at the grant-making organization, and even the grant maker's board members to visit your agency and see your work.

The last piece of advice I can share is don't give up. Pleasant persistence is the coin of the realm in fundraising, the essential currency you need to achieve your goals. I've worked with many different nonprofit and public agencies in which I've heard the refrain, "That won't work. We've tried it before." Sometimes this is true wisdom talking, but many times it's the complaint of a jaded functionary unwilling to try something new. If you keep pushing ahead in your fundraising and follow the steps I've outlined, you can succeed and win the funds your agency needs. And when that happens, Christmas Day will have arrived for you.

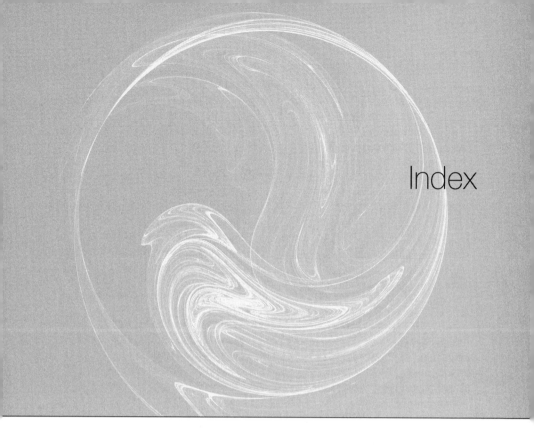

Index